Top Mistakes of Parents

A Guide of Common Parenting Mistakes

Guru Gaurav Arya

ISBN 978-93-5559-170-8
© Guru Gaurav Arya 2021
Published in India 2021 by Pencil

A brand of
One Point Six Technologies Pvt. Ltd.
123, Building J2, Shram Seva Premises,
Wadala Truck Terminal, Wadala (E)
Mumbai 400037, Maharashtra, INDIA
E connect@thepencilapp.com
W www.thepencilapp.com

Author biography

Guru Gaurav Arya is an Indian Astrologer and researcher. He has been practicing astrology since 2007. Now, after completing many cases, providing Astrological Services in the world. At the beginning of their career, he was a Mechanical Engineer. After the completion of Engineering Projects, he started Astrology Consulting. Now, The Guru Gaurav Arya is a leading name in Indian Astrology. He wrote many books on spirituality; he explained the spiritual systems in his books.

Guru Gaurav Arya has a lot of pupils from the world who always get guidance from him. The Chief Minister awarded guru many times at Uttarakhand. He is continuously writing self-help, motivational, fiction books. In 2018, Guru wrote his first book, "Shree Shani Samhita," the best book on lord Shani dev, a Hindu deity. After that, he wrote many spiritual books on Indian spirituality.

Guru Gaurav Arya

Astrologer & Researcher Design Engineer, B. Tech M.E

Author: Motivational, Spiritual, Self-Help

Follow the Author: Twitter:@gurugauravrya,

Instagram:gurugauravaryaofficial

CONTENTS

Epigraph

"EVERY CHILD HAS A UNIQUE QUALITY;

JUST PARENTS NEED TO IDENTIFY THEM."

Acknowledgements

Top Mistakes of Parents

A complete Guide for Parenting

By

GURU GAURAV ARYA

(Astrologer & Researcher, Life Coach, Counselor)

First Edition: 2022

Introduction

The purpose of this book is how you can do good parenting. As everybody knows, today's time is changing at a fast speed. And now everything is going challenging for everyone, in relationship-related matters. One of these is the relationship between parents and children. When someone becomes a parent, they think many things in their minds and feel too happy. They feel anxious about their child as well.

But now the question is that this worry required? So, I think yes! Because children are the mirror of parents' karma. As per the Puranas and Shastras, children are our ancestors or our past birth connection. Many things stress parents and children in between life, like misunderstanding, generation gap, ego, etc. However, this book depends on my personal experience and incidents around me. So, I'll endeavor to help all parents ask for a promising career and be apprehensive about their child's life. Maybe this book hurts your feelings because toxic parents never understand their faults. As an astrologer, I witnessed many family cases that parents are unhappy with their children. Children are also dissatisfied with their parents.

So, I think somewhere is something problematic between children and parents. What do you think? Are parents like a god? So, it is true because the creator of anything is God for their creation, but the second question is that humans cannot become God because humans are the idol of mistakes.

And the second thing is that, if the problem is occurring, something somewhere is wrong, so I think we should work on their parenting. I'll try to discuss with you to make you happy by using this book that you will face no issues about parenting. I have seen dedicated parents to children, yet they met concerns about their parenting. Many things may be responsible for that, like over-care or possessiveness towards children. After many experiences dealing with such instances in various families, I decided to share the "Top mistakes of parents" named book. I have mentioned twenty common mistakes inside this book that are common in society. This book will be an enlightening prospect for both existing and future parents. I have noted many family conversations for better understanding, and I hope those conversations will help. So, come and start a journey with me to correct your ways where possible and become good at parenting.

>>CHAPTER 1<<

TOO EARLY OR DELAYED PARENTHOOD

The purpose of Marriage is to build a new family, and children are a prominent part of successful marriage life. They face many issues, such as a boring lifestyle, jealousy from other couples, taunts from family members, and irritability. Because if you have everything like a Distinguished Career & Good wealth and good name and fame in society and not have children, then you will think, why I am earning and for whom? If you are a parent, then congratulations, and also you have the significant responsibility to make another future and your career. So now two things are there. The first is, earlier parenthood second is late Parenthood. The question is also important what the perfect age of childbearing is? So I would like to say it depends upon your health, financial conditions, & partners' understanding.

There are two factors of Parenthood which are in general condition.

- **Delayed Parenthood.**

- **Early Parenthood.**

You cannot become a parent without children, so Parenthood's first step; after that, Parenting will come. Before proceeding, we should know well about the difference between Parenthood and Parenting.

Parenting will come when you have become a parent. Parenting involves rearing a child. It includes the techniques, methods, and skills you will use in raising your child. Concepts of bathe, feed, and soothing your baby are all part of Parenting. Providing direction and instilling family values are parenting tasks once your child is older, teaching values, discipline, and responsibility.

Parenthood, A person enters Parenthood when they become a parent. It most commonly happens when their child is born, but it can also occur through adoption, marrying, or becoming a partner to someone with children. It involves the role you are taking, as a mother or father and as a co-parent with your partner.

The first forms of the word Parenthood come from the 1850s. The suffix -hood indicates a state or condition—in this case, the state of being a parent. It's used in the same way in words like motherhood, fatherhood, adulthood, and childhood. In a few words, we can say that Parenting is the process of growing and educating a child from birth until maturity, while Parenthood is the state of being a parent.

Delayed Parenthood.

During the astrology practice, I saw that couples had completed many years of Marriage and had not become a parent so far. I saw many people lead this matter efficiently and say this age is not perfect for child planning, whereas they had crossed 35 years of their lives. With this mentality, many issues can occur like medical problems, health problems, etc. Today's the daily routine and diet of persons is not good, many reasons for health problems like pollution, stress, hectic schedule and other many factors.

So, I understand that a career has its place and family has a different role in life, and the couple who understand this will never feel lonely until the end of life. Everyone seeks wealth and a career to enjoy life, like that children are a crucial part of life to enjoy the life.

I mean career, Marriage, and children; these things relate to each other. You are making a career and assets because you want a luxury life and insurance for your future, but who will take over your assets after you? Your children. So you can think children are an essential part of life.

So the first thing is that timing is significant for child planning. Late planning can kill your dreams of happiness in the later stage of life. So do not make a mistake like that. The perfect timing of Parenthood will give you a good life.

What are the significant issues you may face if you delay a Parenthood?

That is an age factor.

Now try to understand how?

Suppose you married about 40 years of age and your partner is approximately equal to you in age, and then if you plan for the baby after two years of Marriage.

So what is your age right now?

That is 42-43 years, and then you may become the parents in 35 years. So if you are in a joint family and your mother and father are living with you, you can feel comfortable because your parents have experienced and cared for your baby.

But if you are not in a joint family or a couple living single, then this situation is very typical for you. If both are working personalities, you will find a maid or baby care center for the baby. Maybe this step is not suitable for your baby's future, as you know very well. Otherwise, one person will compromise with their career to care for the baby. But my main point is the age factor because, when you become a parent then your age is 43 (as we have above assumed) and your child age is a few months, but when your age is 50 years old, then your child is only five years old, and when you are in the age of senior citizen, your child would be 17 years old. And if you will do the Marriage of your children about in 32 years, what would be your age? I think 75 to 76.

How can you support your grandson or granddaughter? At this age, you may face many health issues and other problems that are not good for your children and your grandchildren. And how can you care for your grandchildren as you also need more care? Now time to read some case studies.

Case Study

In 2016, a doctor who got married at 38 and was trying for family planning; failed because of some medical issues. Then what? He treated the same medical problems, but he could not become a parent. He got frustrated and held the hand of God and then spent many things on astrologers, worship, and other things. After a long time, they become parents with medicine and God's blessings, but the parents are 43 years old, and now you can understand what they face in their upbringing. If they had planned and felt any medical problems at the right age, they would have had enough time to seek medical care. In old age, they will touch on many issues in Parenting. They will feel less energy, and children want their parents should be energetic and healthy always because children have their world and their parents are superheroes of that world.

Too Early Parenthood

Early Parenthood is good, but too early Parenthood is not good. When couple bonds in a marriage relationship, they need time to know each other. Women need some time to understand the family. If a woman knows her partner very well, her partner will support her during the pregnancy. This condition also applies to the family because family members also help the couple. Early Parenthood may have more destructive consequences because of its features; pregnancy is more often unexpected, the family unit rarely establishes at the time of conception, and the young parents are at a critical point of life.

What are the harmful points of Early Parenthood? Early Parenthood harmed educational attainment and employment.

- **Miscarriages.**

- **Unplanned Baby.**

- **Sudden load of parenting.**

- **They need more maturity.**

- **Loss of Education.**

- **Health Problems.**

- **Disturbances in sexual life.**

- **Career loss.**

- **The burden of more responsibility.**

- **Financial problems.**

Early Parenthood Facilitate Economic Achievement?

It is the opportunity cost explanation and is potentially relevant for men and women considering early Parenthood. Early Parenthood decreases the opportunities to develop human capital or work experience, as growing children is costly and time-consuming. However, if a young father does not accept responsibility for his child, his opportunity costs are unaffected by fatherhood.

Will Early Parenthood disturb your personal life?

In the primary stage of Marriage, life partners need time to enjoy life. They want to build a house first. After that, they plan for a baby. They wish to the excursion to enjoy life. But in the case of early Parenthood, they will move towards the kid responsibility. So they will lose their personal life as they want.

>>CHAPTER 2<<

CHILDREN ARE THE MIRROR OF YOUR KARMA

I remember the adage, "As you sow, so shall you reap." it is true. If you are not doing good for society, this Karma will show inside your children.

What is Karma?

Karma is an action and reaction. If we show goodness, we will reap goodness. Regarding spiritual development, Karma is all about what a person has done, is doing, and will do. Karma is rational about punishment or reward. It makes people responsible for their lives and how they treat other people.

The process of action and reaction on all levels—physical, mental, and spiritual—is Karma. One must pay attention to thoughts because thought can make karmas—good, bad, and mixed.

The Universal Karmik Law says, depending on the karmic link between the souls involved, the child can befriend, foe, debtor, creditor, advisor, or indifferent to the parents.

Some children bring happiness, success, and wealth to their parents because they are born to deliver to their parents. That is the karmic debt they have to pay off. Some children cause unending misery to their parents, costing them time, money, anguish, and worries because that is the relationship they have to fulfill with their parents. Unless we know the results of our karmas, how can we say who is afflicting who? We accept that nature is delivering the right results for our karmic debts.

In Indian Astrology, many opinions tell how your children will become in the future? It depends upon your current life or past life, Karma.

Suppose a couple does not have children so far means they punished other children or did something wrong with another kid. That's why they are facing an issue. Second things suppose you did not care about your parent, so may be possible your children also do not care about you. It is called the Mirror of Karma.

As I am an astrologer, I want to give some astrological reasons. They will speak about your Karma. You can read your birth and can see your Karma for your parenting.

In Vedic Astrology, the 5th House shows the Kids and their lifestyle. If someone is childless, childless yoga will be inside the native's Birth Chart, and you know the Birth chart very well shows your Karma.

Know, How Spiritual Karma will work, and how can you find it in the birth chart?

Some Astrology Opinions I'm giving here.

1. The 5th House and its Lord are hemmed between Jupiter and malefic, or when karaka Jupiter has a malefic association, the native will suffer child loss.

2. If the lord or ruler of 1st, 5th, and 7th Houses or Bhavas and Jupiter are afflicted because of the aspect or occupation by Malefic or when with them, a similar fate can be experienced.

3. The 5th lord without beneficial aspect is weak, with a malefic in the 5th House.

4. Lords of the 6th, 8th, or 12th are with the 5th lord or without benefic conjunction or aspect.

5. Moon and Jupiter are placed in evil houses or lords of the 5th from birth ascendant, and Chandra or Moon Lagna is in evil houses.

6. Mars and Saturn aspect the 5th House. The weak lord of the 2nd or the 7th House sits in the 5th House.

7. The 5th House Lord is with Mars and Rāhu.

8. The 5th House Lord and Jupiter lie with Mars.

9. Sun and Venus are with the 5th lord.

10. A malefic is in the 1st, 1st lord is in the 5th. The 5th lord is in the 3rd, and the Moon is in the 4th House.

11. The 5th lord malefic and in the 12th House from the Ascendant.

12.Ketu placed in 9th house with the moon.

12. Ketu lies in the 5th House from the Ascendant or the 5th lord.

Scorpio, Virgo, Taurus, and Leo are barren Rashis. Indian Vedic astrology suggests that if Saturn lies in the 12th House (8th from the 5th), it denies children to Sagittarius Ascendants. It is also the case of Cancer and Saturn natives in the 12th House. Based on astrological conclusions, Sagittarius and Cancer Ascendants have Mars as the 5th House Lord.

However, I am not here to teach astrology; I am showing this information because how can we understand parents' Karma in kids by using astrology?

There is another adage that Karma definitely will come back. The above line is compelling for everyone, and science is also saying about the above line that is "Every Action having Reaction," and this line also applies in parenting. If you misbehave with someone's kids, the bad things are your Karma, and definitely, this bad Karma will come back to you; the Karma can be changed, but your bad Karma will be back definitely. So, Karma will decide which type of children you will get.

Now the question is that where is the mistake in parenting? The mistake is in your Karma that you will perform after the Marriage or before. Your Karma will be back as your children. After the wedding, every couple tries to become a parent. So in this period, if couples do bad Karma with another one, those are the bad Karma of the new couple.

I am giving a case study to understand the better.

A new couple married a month ago and settled in a metro city and took a flat for rent to live there. Another family lives in the next flat of the couple. The family has a small kid, and he is very stubborn and naughty. When the new couple introduced the family, they felt uncomfortable because of the mischievous kid because the naughty kid was making disturbed again and again.

After few days

Both women are talking to each other, and a naughty kid is playing. Suddenly, Kid broke the table lamp, which was very costly. The new lady generates a negative image towards the naughty child. And in her mind, she plans to punish the naughty child.

One day in the absence of his mother, the lady slapped to naughty child and shouted to him, that does not make a sound here. I'm not too fond of your sound.

The kid was crying, and after some time, the child told everything to his mother. After this matter, there was a distance between the families.

After a few years, new couples move to another city, and now they are changing doctors day by day because they are not becoming parents. So, I think their Karma comes against him. I have many examples like this, so do not inappropriate behavior with the other child. If you conduct improperly with another child, this Karma will return to you. I'll say to everyone, do not make unacceptable behavior the animal's child as well.

>>CHAPTER 3<<

GIVING MORE IMPORTANCE TO OWN FEELINGS

The Word Feeling is a very required terminology for every human. Yes, you are thinking right. Without feelings, no relation can run, or one can love without feeling. Our Feelings are used to bond with others, and feelings make us surrender to the situation.

For Example, every mother has feelings for their child, and the father also has feelings for their child. So this feeling is making a bond for each other. According to a Sanskrit aphorism, **"Ati Servter varjayet"** means the excess of everything is not suitable for us. Over-felling can make you sad.

But I am not talking about the over feeling for anyone, and here I want to say that caring for children's feelings is a must for good parenting. But sometimes, I saw many parents are not caring about children's feelings in front of their feelings.

For Example, if there is only one cooler for air in a room, and parents are saying we will use this cooler and the children will be warm, that is not fair. In this Example, parents show self-love and do not feel for their children's requirements. However, they can adjust with Childs. Like this Example, many examples are parents in society. Many parents are live in warm temperatures and provide cooling facilities to their children.

Now we will understand what powerful feelings are?

Which will apply to children.

SAD	HAPPY	HURT
Upset	*Joyful*	*Jealous*
Depressed	*Grateful*	*Anger*
Frustrated	*Party*	*Down*
Dismayed	*Overfull*	*Losses*

The above chart shows the three types of feelings mentioned, with particular conditions.

First is Sad

If you are sad, then maybe many reasons are there, like upset, because your wish not fulfilled today or many reasons may be. So, you will feel upset, and now your behavior can jumpy, and your child comes near you and asks for something, then you can shout at them and say to them to move from there. So in this situation, I suggest that you give more importance to your feelings and not prioritize child feelings.

Now see the conversation to understand better.

Conversation (3.0)

A Father depressed and sitting silent. His son enters the room and asks for money for a school project.

Son: Daddy, I want some money for my school project.

Father: No Reply, Silent.

Son: Daddy! Listen to me, what am I saying to you?

Father: Yes, get out, do not disturb me.

Son: It's urgent. I am taking part in the event of school.

Father: What do you want? (Rudely).

Son:I want some money.

Father: Get out from here, can't you look? I am in tension. (at yelling).

Son: Aww (Sad),

The son goes away and waits for the father, but the father does not come to the son.

Son also told the mother about their school event, and the mother also gave the irresponsible answer to the son that daddy is in tension, so we cannot say anything to him.

Next Day

Father is going to Office, and Mother is cooking for everyone.

The son feels uncomfortable and hesitates to say anything because he remembers last night's scolding.

Side Effects of this Behave

May many side effects, the child will hesitate to share any feelings with their parents. The child will feel uncomfortable sharing any problem with you. He will find another way to share his issues. Finding someone outside the family may be possible, and that unknown person may harm the child. This anonymous person can misuse the child's feelings. In this situation, care for yourself and your child's feelings.

Second is Happy

In Joyful: If you are happy for some reason and want to enjoy, you should not enjoy drinks with friends. Many peoples enjoy happiness with their friends or with their colleagues. But do you know? In this period, you had forgotten about your Childs and did not share any enjoyment with them. So in this situation, children cannot enjoy themselves with you, and they will face difficulty knowing your feelings.

In Grateful: Always consider your children and your family at any glorious moment. Share your happiness with them.

For Example-You got a promotion in your job profile, so you should credit your child's luck and pray towards them. If you do not want to give credit to them, you can credit your family. The family will get in touch with you more than before by this credit.

At Party: You should not drink in front of children with your friends. This Habit gives you poor results, and your child will never share personal views with you. May they fear you, and also you can lose your respect in the eyes of children.

In Overfull: You should not take over drunk and misbehave with family members. This effect makes you the wrong person in front of the child.

To understand better, let see the conversation.

(Conversation 3.1)

A father got a promotion in the office, and he is celebrating with their friends at home. And the bad thing is that they are enjoying the alcohol. At the party, children are not present because parents are not considering him in their happiness.

In the above image, we can see parents are enjoying the party with their friends. And in the other picture, children are outside and getting bored.

After some time, one child enters the party room, and then he asks something from his parents.

Child: Daddy, I am getting bored.

Father: Why did you come here?

Mother: Go outside and play or watch TV.

Father: Have you not heard?

Child: Ok, I am going out

Father to Friends: Today's kids don't even listen.

This type of case I rarely saw. In the above conversation, we see parents are putting their feelings first. And they are not taking care of children's feelings.

How can this conversation be healthy?

Parents can enjoy themselves with their friends. The parent can enjoy the promotion party, but they should celebrate happiness with the children first. After that, they can go outside with their friends and enjoy themselves. One thing they can also do, they can enjoy a regular party with the children and friends without alcohol.

If they want a cocktail party, they can first enjoy it with the children; after that, they can enjoy it outside the home with friends.

Parents should include the children in every happiness of life, whether this happiness is not related to the children. If they do this, the relationship between children and parents will become strong. Children will also share their joy with their parents, and this system is called the family. Children and friends have a unique position in life. It is bearable once you ignore your friends in your happiness, but it is not sustainable if you forget your family in your joy.

The third Point is hurt.

Many reasons are there who can hurt your child's feelings.

Jealous: I have seen this factor only in a few parents, but this factor is critical. I saw some parents do competitive behavior with their children. For Example, if a child's getting good at any task, so parents say, "we were more experts than you when we were at this age." But this dialog makes you down in front of your children.

Let see the conversation to know better.

(Conversation 3.2)

A child was studying in 10th standard. He got first prize in a school event. The child was delighted and wanted to share this news with their parents, then he came home and said to his parents. The next day, this news will print in every city newspaper.

Child: Mom and Daddy, I got the first position at the school event, and tomorrow my photo and name will print in the newspaper.

Daddy: ok.

Mom: ok.

Child: Mom, do you know, the teacher gave me an appreciation for this work.

Daddy: Ok, no need to be happier. Take your lunch.

Mom: First, take a bath, and I am serving lunch for you.

Child: ok, I am going (Feeling sad).

On the table

Child: Mom, do you know the first time my photo will print tomorrow in the newspaper?

Mom: Who told you?

Child: The teacher told me, and one person also captured my photo.

Daddy: When I was your age, then every week, my name was printed in every city newspaper.

Mom: Ok, stop you both and take your lunch.

Child: Aww (Not Eating and silent).

In the above conversation, what do you think? You think parents are doing competitive behavior with the child. Do you know this type of parent is seldom? But in society, I have seen this type of competitive parent many times. Do you know, this competitive behavior takes place in the mind of parents, and they will do this behavior with everyone in the society, so how can they spare their children?

Do you know this competitive behavior will lose your child's confidence? Yes, I am right, this behavior will lose the self-spirit of your child, from the next time child will never try to share their happiness with you. As I told you before, children want to do everything for appreciation. Children are greedy for appreciation, and if parents will not give appreciation for good work, then why will children try for the task? Motivation and appreciation are booster doses for every child, but quantities should not be excessive. Because if you give over appreciation at every step, the child can become an egoist person. And if you pass over motivation at every step, then the child can irritate by your speech.

Anger: For no reason to do not show your anger to children. It will take you down in front of children. Maybe many reasons can make you angry, like office tension or any other reasons, but in this situation, calm down for your Childs, and do not show anger to your Childs.

This mistake is also notable for some parents, mostly the father, who anger the child without reason. He can shout at a child anywhere and transfer their anger towards them. It is a terrible habit. This type of behavior makes you a devil in the eyes of children. Children will scare of you and never share problems with you. And I told you before if your child is not communicating with you anything, it means something is not good in the child's life. Anger is good at the right place but within a limit, but it is not a good habit if you show your rage without reason.

Same as the above Example, Down and losses are the same. If you are feeling down, so do not put your feeling first. If you have lost anything, do not ignore the child's feelings because the child does not know about your problem.

>>CHAPTER 4<<

PARTIALITY BETWEEN CHILDREN (FAVORITISM)

The word Partiality makes a difference between people, but sometimes this difference will cause a lot of loss of humanity. Parents also discriminate with children, and this Partiality can be between the boy and boy, girl and girl, or girl and boy.

I have seen this discrimination in many places that parents make a difference between the boy and the girl; the boy gets more care, and the girl gets less care. By doing this, tension can arise among the children, going into depression due to stress. Because of the depression, the child will remain silent, not talk to anyone, and not show any interest in studies. That is why it is very wrong to do Partiality among children.

Keep Partiality out of children's minds.

If you go to the market or go to a place where you have to buy anything for the children, do it so that the child does not feel that I have got less and my brother or sister has gained more than me. In this stage, your child will feel distance from you. Maybe they feel very loose. To avoid this thing, use equal good communication to satisfy the children.

We can understand better by this conversation.

A Mother is in the market with their boys. The elder boy's name is Sammy, and the younger boy's name is Jacky. Mother is purchasing some toys for their child. Jacky is a very naughty boy and always in mischief. Both boys want to buy the new toy car.

Conversation (4.0)

Sammy: Mom, I want a novel car of red color, which has a remote control.

Jacky: I also want the same car, mom.

Mother: Jacky, Last time I gave you a novel car, and you have lost it.

Now you will take a simple car without a remote control.

Mother: Sammy, you can choose as per your choice.

Jacky: But mom, Sammy, lost my car.

Sammy: I don't think you should blame me for this.

Mother: Stop your fight, you both of them.

Mother: Jacky, you will not purchase a car for yourself. You can take only a simple toy car, and Sammy, you take your toy car quickly.

Jacky: but Mom, I will not make mischief now.

Mother: I do not want to listen to anything. I will complain to your father.

Jacky: No, I'll not take anything.

Sammy:hahaha, yes, I got it my new car.

Jacky:(Sad and feeling anger and helpless).

What do you think about this conversation?

Is Mother doing well? Because Jacky is a naughty boy, he always breaks the toys and harms everyone, so the mother is not purchasing toys for him. But the mother is buying the toys for the other child. I called this favoritism. If one child is not good, you cannot avoid him, put some conditions in front of him to fulfill his wish like that he will not harm toys anymore. Otherwise, she should not purchase the toys together with the boys. If the mother is watching that boys are fighting for toys, then the mother should cancel the purchasing plan instantly.

Every child has unique skills and hobbies.

I often saw parents expect many things from their children, but children have unique skills. So, you should not apply your expectancy to children. If you are doing it repeatedly, your children will lose their confidence. Also, the child will lose their skill of interest.

Favoritism Suppresses talents

As a parent, when you favor a talented child, this favor will suppress the latent of the less favored child. Because of the lack of encouragement and support, the child will doubt their abilities, hide their talents and true potential.

According to psychologists, an emotionally healthy child will want to display his talents to you and learn faster. Always encourage your kids to display their talents and not praise or encourage only one child. Encourage all the children to perform to the best of their abilities.

How can favoritism suppress talent?

By reading this conversation, we can understand better.

A family has three children, one boy and two girls. The boy's name is Sandy, and the girl's name is Eddy and Joya. The parents love Eddy more because she is adorable and innocent. But Sandy is a very naughty boy, and nobody likes him because of his mischief.

Joya is a very reserved type of girl. She has no extra time for unnecessary things. Eddy is not good at studying and is a lazy kind of girl. But Sandy is a talented footballer at school, achieved many rewards for incredible playing.

But his parents do not have any respect for his game. Parents think he is wasting time in football.

Let see the conversation about how parents are suppressing Sandy's talent.

Conversation (4.1)

Parents: Sandy, we are coming from your school. There was a parents' meeting today.

Sandy: Ok, what happened there?

Parents: Your teacher was saying you are average in all subjects. It would be best to work hard to achieve the excellent percentile in school.

From today, stop sports and focus on your study.

Sandy: Yes, I'll do more study and try my best, but I have more interest in football.

Parents: Your sports teacher said that you work hard in school sports.

Sandy: Yes, I'll achieve the next trophy soon.

Parents: Trophy will not give you the excellent percentile.

Parents: No, First get a good percentile, then think about football.

Parents: No, focus only on your study.

Sandy: But mom and daddy, Eddy is doing her hobbies with the study, and she has no sound report card so far.

Parents: Eddy is sincerer than you. She can do everything. If not today, then tomorrow will do.

Sandy: I want to perform well in football games.

Parents: No, you can not do it. Invariably we get complaints about your mischief.

Sandy: Aww (Feeling Sad).

In the above conversation, we can notice that the parents are ignoring the weakness of Eddy and not saying anything to her. But they are suppressing the talent of Sandy because they are not interested in sports. It is the favoritism that is burying the talent.

If parents are not interested in games or do not know of the football game, they should not stop their child from playing the game, whereas his sports teacher promotes the boy.

Parents can use the condition for the boy if you perform in study well, then we will support you in your sports.

Shy away from society

Children want to perform a confident demeanor at social events and gatherings to wish and greet the elders and respond to conversations. A less-favored child may be shy and not respond appropriately. As kids grow up, they lack social skills because of self-confidence. According to experts, less favored children may believe that they cannot become good people all over life.

Emotional effects

People rarely forget that they were not treated fairly by their parents. The neglected children may develop hatred towards the parent who displayed favoritism. Also, such children are more likely to exhibit aggression and inappropriate behavior in their schools and with siblings. The lack of parental affirmation and affection may leave a void in their lives that they never fill. Children can also exhibit signs of depression very early in life.

Stress and self-esteem

Displaying partiality towards a child can cause unrequited stress. The feeling or perception of being the less favorite can hurt a child's self-esteem. For instance, labeling one of your children as smart or intelligent may lead to unnecessary and unhealthy competition among the kids, where one would continuously try to put the other down. In adulthood, the less favored child may still lack self-esteem and may not perform well in their work lives.

How can a child come under stress because of favoritism?

Let's come and see the conversation.

Conversation (4.2)

A family has two children, and both are boys. One boy has a dark complexion named Sam, and the second boy's name is Mac, and his skin color is fair. Parents are also good-looking, but they always comment on Sam because of his dark complexion. Because of this, Mac is dominating on SAM.

One day, the father is going to the party with a colleague, boys also want to go with the father.

SAM: Daddy, I'll come with you. I want to see your office party.

MAC: Yes, Daddy, I also want to go with you.

Father: No, you both do your study. I'll go there alone.

Mother: If they want to go with you, take both of them with you.

Father: No, it is a reputed party, at the party, all are my bosses. I can not take any risk.

Mother: Ok, as you wish.

Suddenly, a mobile ringed of the father.

Father: Yes, Mr. John, are you coming to the party?

John: Yes, I am coming with my wife and son.

Father: Ok, great, I will also come with my family. See you at the party, Mr. John.

Now Father said to the mother, can you come with me to the party? The mother refuses the offer and gives an excuse for the headache.

Father: Ok,

Father: MAC, you join me, change your dress, and be gentlemen.

Then SAM says to daddy, and I want to come with you.

Father: No, you will stay here with your mother.

Mother: No, I am ok, you can go.

Father: No can see you are not looking fine.

SAM: But daddy, you are going with the MAC.

Father: Yes, MAC deserves it, and you will look different at the party.

MAC: But Daddy.

Father: No, take care of your mother's headache.

SAM: hahaha (laughing).

After reading the above conversation, can you imagine how SAM was to feel?

Yes, you are right! It is ok if the SAM could not understand his father's intention. Otherwise, he will be in depression. In his mind, many questions would be circulating. He will lose their self-confidence. He will try to run away from himself.

He will share nothing with other people. Otherwise, he will become aggressive and try to harm himself or another. So do not do Favoritism with anyone. Every child is the creation of God, and God never makes mistakes. Our Mistakes force others to make the mistakes.

How can we control Favoritism?

I am giving a Few Points that can be necessary to you.

- Avoid the matters which can make a difference between children.

- Always make behavior balance between children.

- Learn to live without parents

- Do not spend too much on children's toys or things that are not good for children.

- Always share equally and adequately between children.

- Don't praise the other child too much in front of one child

- Do not force copying one child to another child.

- Ensuring children's health is always fit means care of children should be similar.

- If you are angry with children, so do not skip your formalities.

- When children need you, and then always help them.

- Do not talk to children for selfish reasons.

- Don't be tempted to do something.

- Avoid things that can make fights between children—for Example, dresses or toys.

- Do not shout at only one child, shouting in a manner at all children.

>>CHAPTER 5<<

NOT UNDERSTANDING THE CHILDREN'S NEEDS & DEMANDS

First, we should see the difference between Need and Demand. As we know, at every age, the person's needs will change. Like that, children will ask many things as time varies. So parents should always be ready to know the needs of their children. I know, each demand of children we can not complete. But we should be aware of their needs.

Needs: it means necessary things which are compulsory for children.

- Food

- Clothes

- Love

-

Safety

- Education

- Health Care

- Parents Support

Food: For Every Step of life, good food requires every child. Without food, we cannot go ahead for life, as everyone knows good food is the strength of good health.

Clothes: Clothes are also a basic need for every child, but they can vary from child to child. Maybe some parents are wealthy and can buy costly clothes, and someone's parents are incapable of doing this. But every parent should know the value of clothes for their children do not buy expensive dresses. You can adjust as per your standard. But the main thing is that you should know about child dressing sense.

Love: Love is the purest form in the world. After all the above needs, every child deserves love from parents because love gives strength to the child. Even when your kids have disobeyed, angered, frustrated, and rebelled against you, show them you love them and that you'll always love them.

Safety: The child must feel safe and sound with their parents in society after the basic survival needs like shelter, food, clothing, medical care, and protection from harm. Parents should care for and provide safety from road vehicles, security from harmful things, etc. When the child is small, he has no sense of safety. He does not know what is secure and not. It is the responsibility of parents to protect the child should not do negligence in safety. I saw many parents are very irresponsible about their children. They always live in themselves.

I am sharing a conversation that can tell you better.

Conversation (5.0)

A couple is going on the road with a newborn baby. A newborn baby is on the trolley, the mother is moving the trolley, and the father is beside the trolley. Suddenly, the father's mobile rings, and he accepts the call and starts talking on the mobile. Father has stopped the walk and continued talking on the phone.

Mother has also stopped walking. Mother is staring at the dresses on the opposite side of the road.

Mother: Please take care of the baby. I am coming back in a few minutes. "Said to the husband."

Husband: Ok (He is busy on mobile).

The trolley is sliding from the footpath, and the father is busy on the mobile. Suddenly the trolley comes in front of a car, and the vehicle applies the brake. Suddenly, the crowd gathers, and the mother comes back fast towards the trolley. Mother saves the baby as soon as possible.

The crowd speaks badly to the parents, that if you can not care for your children, then why are you walking here? After this incident, mother and father debated with each other.

Mother: You can not take care of your baby.

Father: When you knew I was talking on the phone, why did you go there?

And They have started arguments.

So, what do you think, whose fault? I think both are irresponsible. Parents did not take the child seriously. They are thinking only for themselves. This type of Parent cannot provide safety to children.

How could they avoid this mistake?

If the father is on mobile and the baby is with the mother, then the mother should not leave the child alone with the father because his husband is already busy.

Education: Beyond any doubt, your kids get the leading conceivable instruction for their future in school, of course, but it is the essential life lessons you give amid the time you spend together. The Education standard can vary as per parents' financial situation, but education is necessary.

Health: Care for good life good health is must, children have less knowledge about their health, or you can say there is no sense in their health. So that, it is the responsibility of parents to know which things do require for child health? For Example, which food suits a child or which food is not? Food should be hygienic and safe to eat. Parents always remember when and which vaccine should give to children for health safety.

Sometimes parents avoid or forget the vaccination. So be constantly alert for this. Let's come and see the conversation to know better.

Conversation (5.1)

One day, a family with two children's names follows Rummy and Rocky; the family goes outside to eat the sandwich. At the sandwich shop, parents ignored the hygiene, and they enjoyed sandwiches a lot. See what's going on.

Father: I wouldn't say I like sandwiches. I will take only ice cream.

Mother: Ok, as you wish.

Rummy: Mom, I'll also take Ice cream.

Mother: Ok, we both take the sandwich.

Next Day.

Mother: Get up, children, get ready for school.

Rocky: Mom, I am not feeling well; I have a pain in my stomach.

Mother: Do not give me an excuse. Get ready soon.

Rocky awakened, and he started to vomit.

Father: What happens? I told you, do not eat sandwiches!

Mother: Nothing to worry about it. Just a gastric, nothing else.

Rocky: I am getting loose motion.

Mother: Do not worry, I am preparing a home remedy for you.

Father: Ok, do not go to school today. I am going to the Office.

Father said to mother, "I am going to the office, take care of him." Rocky comes into the room and lies down on the bed. Rummy told to mother, "Mom, Rocky is in fever."

Mother: Just a minute. I am coming to give him a home remedy.

Rocky is feeling uncomfortable.

Mother: Rocky, get up, take this lemon and rock salt juice.

Rocky took the juice; he went to the toilet again and again. His condition is getting worse.

At the noon

Mother is going to the medical store for some medicine. She took some anti-gastro pills.

She gives medicine to rocky, but there is no relief to Rocky.

In the evening time

Father came from the Office and asked for Rocky's health.

Father: What happened?

Mother: I am giving treatment to him. He will get well soon.

Father: I think rocky got infected from eating a sandwich.

Mother: I do not think so because I was eating too, but I am fit and fine.

Father: I cannot argue with you. The reason is a sandwich.

Mother: No, I see what you mean, but I'm not entirely convinced.

Father: Ok, do as you want to do. (With helpless tone).

Rocky is trying to sleep, and now his condition is worse.

Rummy: Ok, mom and daddy, stop your fight and call to doctor. Rocky's health is going down.

After this matter, the doctor came and gave treatment to Rocky. And doctor advised avoiding street foods that are not hygienic.

So, what do you think after reading this conversation?

I think parents are too irresponsible; they are not alert about their health.

They could avoid the problem by using the two steps.

When the father was eating ice cream, the father should have stopped the family from purchasing the sandwiches. Otherwise, he should have searched for another hygiene shop for sandwiches.

The mother had not opposed to the unhygienic food as well. She did not think once about the family.

Parents Support: Parents' support means parents should support children in every step of life. Mostly in career choice and activity of life. But parents should always keep positive things. Reinforcement should be positive.

The word support is already tremendous. Because in life, everyone needs support. Supporting each other is called life. And with parents, children always expect from the parents for support.

But sometimes parents make mistakes to support their children, but how?

Let's come and read the conversation.

Conversation (5.2)

A son (Ramu) is going outer of the city for a job, and he is new for the job and does not have sufficient money, but his father is a good businessman in the town and has good money, but he is a stingy type person. Let's see what happens.

Ramu: Daddy, I am going tomorrow for my joining.

Daddy: Ok, fine, enjoy your life, my son.

Mother: Dear son, I've packed your bag. I think it will be cold there, so which blanket should I put in your bag?

Father: No need to take the blanket with you from home; purchase from there.

Ramu: Ok, (Watching face of mother).

And Ramu goes to the city, joins the job, and struggles to settle there. One Day, Ramu Called his father.

Ramu: How are you, daddy?

Daddy: I am fine. How did you call us today?

Ramu: Daddy, I live on the rental property; I want to purchase my flat here to save my rent charges.

Daddy: Ok, you can purchase, no problem, it is good, earn and enjoy your life.

Ramu: Daddy, I have fallen short of some money.

Daddy: You can take a loan from the bank. I have no money right now because I will purchase a new car.

Ramu: Ok, daddy (feeling helpless).

Daddy: You are In job now arrange yourself.

Ramu:I have arranged, but a few amounts are going down.

Ramu asks for help (support) from his father in the above conversation because he asks for some amount, not the entire amount. So, the father should come in front and should have supported the son. Because the son is not demanding the money, the son asks for support.

Father can support the son, whereas he is not supporting him, giving excuses for the car. It is a big mistake of the parent because he breaks the son's confidence and pulls the son's leg.

Demand: It means unnecessary things, which are not compulsory for children.

In the above part, we have discussed the needs necessary for every child. But when time goes by, and kids come out from the family and see the world, they will learn many things via society and friend circles. After learning many things outside the home, they will ask the parents and teachers many things. The questions may vary as per the requirement of living standards in society or school. When the child learns many things, their mind will expand day by day. After expanding memory, many questions will generate in the children's minds, which will create the demand. Now the game will start with the parents, as per the age of children, this demand will change.

For Example, the first time, a kid goes to society's garden with their father. Then the child will see many other children playing different games. Now the two conditions can come towards you.

1.A child can demand quickly to you he wants the ball, football, or other games.

2.On the first day, He does not ask for anything from you.

Now I'll predict something about your child.

If your child comes in the first condition, you can say your child is active and too stubborn. So you need to take care of him smoothly. If you constantly complete his demand on the spot, you can face some issues with your child in the future. You can give him a diplomatic answer about their demand.

Now the thing is that, how can you give a diplomatic answer?

 I have two ideas for that. I consistently applied to my son, Triyansh.

1.My dear baby (Language should be polite because you are in society with child) you are so small for this game (Demand) we can wait for some days, and then we will play together.

2.My dear baby, this game or thing (demand) is not suitable for our standard. We will play a more effective event that will suit our standards.

3.If you failed in the above ideas, then you can go out from there and change the location immediately. And try to convince a child or divert the child's mind.

But I suggest you should not complete the child's demand on the spot.

It would help if you took a few days to understand the child's behavior because the child was demanding as per the seeing of society.

If Kid comes in the second condition.

Here, notice the behavior of the child, mainly health, mind, and security or phobia. Maybe the child is shy, so you need to understand the child's behavior. If a child's health is perfect, then I'll predict your child is intelligent and caring for you. In the future, he will do something for society.

From time to time, the demand for children will change. So always remember, first you should notice the child's behavior and then search why and from where this demand is generating? Most probably, children's needs develop from the friend circles. So you should know very well the child's friend circle. Where your children are going and how much time they spend with friends. Some Times we should understand the demand. Maybe the request of the child is genuine. Because when children go out from home and meet with their teachers and other experts, they can see some study material or some electronic gadgets that can help them learn new technology.

>>CHAPTER 6<<

DO YOU SCARE YOUR CHILD

Sometimes we scare our children into obeying orders. That is not fair for our children. Because of this fear, children will lose confidence, and day by day, their morale will get down. There are two types of fears that parents give to their children.

Short Term Scare

When a child is small, he can demand many things from you, and if you feel it would be better not to complete the demand, then we scare him to convince.

For Example,A child is asking to visit a place or wants to go outside the home, and parents do not want to send, then they will say, "Baby outside is a ghost or police," and they will catch you. Some Indian parents say Baba is outside the home. If you go out, then he will grab you. This fear will set in the tiny mind of children, and it will generate a negative image for the relevant character.

So, always try to give genuine reason to the child for convincing. Sometimes this fear is ok but usually not good.

Long Term Scare

I believe it does base on the daring of parents. If parents are not of daring personalities, they will always try to make their children weak. It means this type of parent is not daring in actual life. And if parents realize they are not of daring personalities, but trying to build their child daring, so this is good, it means this type of parent is brave in real life.

Now back to the business, what is a long-term scare? I can say this type of scare is harmful to a child till he is alive. Sometimes this scare does not feel in practical life, but it works like a slow poison. This scare transfer from one person to another person. Many people do not understand why they were scared by situations, fights, tension, stress, job fear, health, expressing views, public phobia, stage phobia, etc. Behind this scare, long-term scared is place. It is easy to understand what long-term scarring is? This scare starts from the youngest age of the person, and this fear enters his mind from childhood.

First Case Study

Suppose a father is going to the market with his child, someone has stolen his purse, then suddenly he watches the policeman, and he becomes hesitant to discuss with him. When the child asks his father to discuss with the policeman, the father says "NO" and replies, "He will ask many things from me; the police will trouble us." After listening to this sound child will lose confidence and feel insecure in the market.

After reading this, what do you think? The image of police is not good in the father's sight? Father scare of the police? Father is hesitating because of the child? There is no above reason, a negative image regarding the police in his mind. The police give trouble, or maybe the father's self-confidence is low. So, in this case, the father did wrong. He should have thought that his child would learn a lot if he handled the situation with the police. Here, the mother can be in the father's place.

So, how can we say this scare is long-term? In the above Case study, the child is going with the father to the market, and now he is ready to see the world with a small mind. So, it depends upon the father what he wants to teach the child. If the father has any weak point, he should try to remove it in front of his child.

Second Case study

I saw that most parents are used to scaring children with slight fright. Someone is not good, and he is shouting at you, then you are not responding or not taking any action on that person. And children are sensing this matter, and when children say to take action on him and your response is like that "No, I can't say anything" or "I cannot do anything, this person is perilous." After this sound, children will lose confidence. They will make a negative image of this.

So, how can you control this difficulty? It can be said to children to go out from there. Say to your children, this person is angry now. You should respond with peace to him. When he becomes tranquil, we will talk to him and take action against him. If you react like that, children will learn how to control a situation. And if you are not responding to anything, instead you are shouting at your children and saying, "Do not give me advice, what should I do?" then the child will feel unsafe. In his mind, many questions will arise. Your respect will also be down in front of children.

Always tackle this situation with confidence because parents are ideal for every child. And do you know? Children expect strength and security from their heroes.

So do not teach children to fear any situation of life. Your brave lessons will always help your children. And I realize if every child will be bold, then our nation also becomes powerful because children are the nation's backbone.

Why should you not scare your children?

- Will lose self-confidence

- Separation anxiety

- Insecurity

Will Lose Self-Confidence

If you always scare your children, your child will lose self-confidence soon. Suppose he is not obeying you, and for this, you are threatening him by a monster. It will cause unnecessary fear in the mind of children. Always give him a simple word to do the work and encourage him, and do not forget to reward him for work.

Read the conversation to understand better.

Conversation (6.0)

A child named Sandy wants to purchase a toy car that he watched on the market last night. He insisted his parents buy the toy car. But his parents want to avoid it. Let see what's going on.

Sandy: Daddy, please get me the car.

Father: Which Car?

Mother: He is asking for Red color car, which is a haunted car. He killed some kids at night.

Father: Oh really!

Sandy: Mom, what is the meaning of haunted?

Mother: Dear son, Haunted means monsters who kill the small kids.

Father: Oh, that is very dangerous.

Mother: Yes, that's why I am not getting you that car.

Sandy: Mom, Monster can kill me as well?

Mother: Yes, he kills boys especially.

Father: Dear Sandy, I think we should not purchase this car.

Mother: When you become elder, then you can buy.

Sandy: That time monster will go away?

Mother: Yes, Sandy.

Father: Yes, you can buy when you become elder.

Sandy: Ok, mom, (in a scary voice).

The whole night, Sandy was thinking about the monster. He could not sleep well.

Next Day.

When he is ready for school, he asks about the monster from the mom.

Sandy: Mom, why the monster was living in red colors' car?

Mother: Because the monster likes the red color.

Sandy: Aww (Scaring from the red color).

From that day onwards, a misconception about the red color in his mind.

He scares by the red color. In his mind always strikes that red color is the color of the monster.

In this conversation, we can see how the mother is telling lies to refuse the one demand of his son. And the crucial thing is that she is scaring his son, and this scare will lose confidence in his son. His son may become psycho, can adopt some superstitions. He can create a scary world around him.

Separation anxiety

I have come across many parents who always say the dialog, "If you don't take food properly, we will not take you along with us."

It is widespread fear in children that the parents give. Sometimes this fear takes the form of a joke, but this joke works as double-sided swords. Fear of separation can take space in the mind of children, and this space can remain for a long time.

See the conversation to understand better.

Conversation (6.1)

The parents are going to the market for shopping, and the child is taking time to get ready. Then what happens.

Mother: Son, get ready soon.

Child: I will not wear these pants, mom.

Father: Wear these pants with no sound.

Mother: Ok, son, you stay here. We both are going shopping, and you stay here alone.

Child: No, I will not stay here alone.

Father: We will leave you alone here, and the monster will consume you.

Parents are making this habit again and again with their children. But the scare of separation was changing as per the situation.

This scare will work instantly, and definitely, the child will obey your order. But this fear will work as a slow poison, which will damage the mental peace of your child.

What are the side effects that will fall on the child?

- The child will always feel inferior.

- The child will feel scared of the separation.

- A child can imagine bad things at night to separate from parents.

- The chemical reaction of his mind will change, and then he can feel some destructive illusions.

- He can be more attached to you.

- He will force you to live with him during school or tuition.

- Maybe the child will lose their emotional balance.

- A child can be downhearted.

- They refuse to be away from home because of fear of separation.

- Repeated nightmares about separation.

- A child can have frequent headaches, stomachaches, or other symptoms when separation's possible from a parent or other loved one.

Insecurity

When children get scared frequently, then the child can get insecure. It will cause emotional insecurity, even in the presence of caretakers. Children will produce beautiful works when they feel secure.

For Example,

If a child is always scared of dark, sound, animals, and weird, he cannot be happy anywhere. He will always feel insecure even though his parents will support him. Because he fears frequently, that's why he will feel insecure.

Read conversation

Conversation (6.2)

Parents are coming from the market at night. Their child was scared from the night.

Father: Dear son, Go ahead.

Son: No, it's dark ahead. I got scaring.

Mother: Do not scare me. I am with you.

Son: No, mom, we will go from the other way.

Mother and father forced to son, but the son is scaring too much. At last, the mother says to the son, you can close your eyes, and I'll pick you up. You can see how much he feels insecure in his parents' presence. Maybe these parents scare their children. That's why he is feeling insecure.

Read conversation

Conversation (6.2)

Parents are coming from the market at night. Their child was scared from the night.

Father: Dear son, Go ahead.

Son: No, it's dark ahead. I got scaring.

Mother: Do not scare me. I am with you.

Son: No, mom, we will go from the other way.

Mother and father forced to son, but the son is scaring too much. At last, the mother says to the son, you can close your eyes, and I'll pick you up. You can see how much he feels insecure in his parents' presence. Maybe these parents scare their children. That's why he is feeling insecure.

>>CHAPTER 7<<

ARE YOU PUTTING YOUR WORKLOAD ON CHILDREN

Yes, you are thinking right. I am talking about your workload, which makes you tired and irritating. Sometimes we put this workload on our children, and the form of load will transform our bodies' capacity. Today, everybody is very busy because everyone wants to perform better in their field. Knowingly, unknowingly, you are putting your work pressure on your children.

Now the thing is that how can we understand this load? Sometimes we are stressed or pressured by any work which can be of home or office. Suddenly, our behave turns into an irritable nature, and suppose that time child is asking for something like food or any other thing. So, immediately you will respond to the child and say you can take yourself or try to avoid it. Now here is a thing essential for everyone, which is rude behavior. You are also transferring your stress to your child if seen, and you are assigning it. So in a way, you are putting your workload on your children.

Now, after the reading of the above few lines, you will say to me, you tell me how to control this situation? However, I am already under stress. Before suggesting an idea, suppose if you shout at your child or make a rude behave with him so that the child can kill his requirement at that time, or the child can cry loudly. In this stage, stress will become doubled. If you love your children too much, you can also get unhappy after the children's reaction. So, I think this is not fair in any way.

How can you manage?

- You can say to your child to wait for some time.

- You should convince the child and tell him your real stress story.

- You should urgently arrange an alternative thing for your child.

- I always follow the best way to order children to go outside and say play with friends. (in case the requirement is not of food)

- If your child is not small in age, you can involve him in your work but not in stress.

- Give him a task and tell him that maa or papa is doing homework, and you should also do your assignment simultaneously.

Meanwhile, you need to divert the mind of children from the requirement of children as soon as possible if you feel it would be better to avoid fulfilling the condition at that time. So, this situation will come only when your child is not elder.

Now we will see how we can control the situation if your child is older.

In this stage, how you are putting the workload on children, some parents force children to work for money, and they are free from work, which is not fair. I think that is the top mistake of parents. So do not do this, always support children for study and other skills.

Sometimes parents look for their comfort and always force them to work at home or small domestic things, which is terrible. I am not saying that you should not give domestic work to your child, but only if necessary and without the loss of education. Do you know your workload is also affected your child?

The overall research suggests that working parents raise more successful kids. Because those parents thought more for their children, but sometimes due to over workload parents makes a mistake.

But how do they make a mistake? Read conversation.

Conversation (7.0)

A family has a girl named Sanky. Her father and mother both are working in a company. Most of the time, Sanky stays alone after school. Her parents have very little time for her. And when her parents come back home, even then, they keep busy with their work because her parents have a heavy workload of projects.

See what happens?

Mother: Sanky, how's your study going on?

Father: Dear Sanky, I hope you perform well this year.

Sanky: Yes, daddy, but I am facing some issues in math.

Mother: ok, will see you later.

Sanky: But mom

Father: Ok, Sanky, now do your study, we have some work to do.

Mother and father are doing their work. Suddenly, the project manager calls the father and mother in the conference call and scolds both. The manager said, "I want to work on the time limit, so I want tasks from you in a given time."

After the call, parents felt too depressed, and they started working diligently. Suddenly, Sanky comes into the room.

Sanky: Mom, I do not want to go to school tomorrow.

Mother: But Why?

Father: Ok, do not go.

Sanky: I want to go to the zoo with you.

Mother: No, Dear, We are busy with their work.

Father: Do not disturb us and go to your room and do your study.

Sanky: No, I'll go zoo.

Mother: Go and do your study (yelling).

Father: What is the problem? Neither peace in the house nor outside.

Sanky ran to the room (feeling sad).

In the above conversation, you will say the parents are under stress; that's why they behave like this. Where are they putting their workload on children? Yes, you are right, but if you read deeply, they are transferring their working stress to the child, and I am saying that this stress is like a workload because the source of stress is parents' workload.

As demonstrated by the above conversation, when parents came home, they asked about the child's study, and the speaking tone was formal. It means parents are good and thinking for child's education. But they are making mistakes during the pressure of workload.

They are hurting their child's feelings, and they do not understand after this behavior, the tension will not reduce, pressure will increase.

But the question is that how they can manage this problem?

In the pressure of any work, try to reduce the problem. Give the genuine reason to the child, or you can give the task to the child as well.

Some Time I have seen some parents makes fake promises to convince that time child. This fake promise can kill the slight feeling of a child. As you can see in the conversation, the father used a word that is heart breakable word for the child (Neither peace in the house nor outside). Do not use this type of word in family. These types of terms generate an Inferiority complex in the mind of children.

>>CHAPTER 8<<

NO GUIDANCE FOR THE FUTURE

To build the future of the children is the responsibility of every parent. Schools are secondary, but parents are the primary teacher of children. Most parents are busy improving their careers, and they forget about the child's future in this hurry. You will have to understand the child's interest, and you need to search about this interest and take help from others and then give advice to the children. You can not impose anything on a child usually.

I know money earning is necessary for every family to survive in society. Thus, it would be best if you understood this. After some time child will also help you.

How do parents make mistakes during the guidance of children?

- They are busy in the office work or business.

- They are not spending time with the child.

- At the time of career selection, parents are not showing interest.

- Not taking reports from teachers and friends.

- Not trying to know the problem of children.

- Only projecting goals on children for marks.

By the way, every parent tries to make their child's future bright. But in the course of life survival, they will face many situations, and in this situation, some parents could not give proper time to their children—age matters to provide advice for the future. In childhood, children need a way of living and necessary guidance. And when time moves ahead, the direction change from time to time. Parents should guide why and how outdoor games are good for us in the age of playing. And in the period of education and knowledge, parents should show why and how education is beneficial for good nation power. Parents should also teach their children about religion and spirituality because this knowledge will help them become good human beings.

I am dividing this guidance into three steps, keeping the age factor in mind.

1. Childhood Age

2. Schooling Age

3. College Age

Childhood Age- Parents should guide why education must be for us? And why are we spending time in education? Because education is our treasure. We can achieve anything with the help of education. At this age, if you succeed in filling these words in the mind of the children, then the child will never come back to see the failure of life.

In childhood, most children's minds attract to games and useless activities. So parents will play a vital role in guiding the children. But this time is for the foundation of primary education.

How do parents make mistakes? See in the below conversation.

Conversation (8.0)

A Family has three children, the father is a shopkeeper, and the mother is a housewife. One day, a relative comes to the home. He is a distant relative, a teacher in a government school. Let see what happens?

Relative: How are you, Elder brother? (To Shopkeeper Father).

Father: We are fine, just spending time on shop.

Father: Comes and take your seat. Would you take tea?

Relative: No, I'll take a glass of water.

Relative after taking water. What else? Where are the kids?

Father: where they will go, just playing inside.

Relative: Come, children, take your gifts.

Children come near the relative and get gifts.

Relative: In which class do you study?

Children: We are not going to school so far.

Relative: ok, play children.

Relative to Father

The elder brother, one thing is to tell me, why are you not sending children to school?

Father: What is the age now, just 3 to 4 years old.

It is a time of play and enjoyment.

Relative: But you should think about their future as well. It is the time of the foundation of education. In elder age, the child will bother you to go to school because he will feel uncomfortable in the lower class.

Relative: What is your future planning for children?

Father: Nothing to do, unique. They will run my business.

Relative: Ok elder brother, sorry to bother you.

You can see this parent have not any plan for children future. He is not giving any guidance to children. At the age of schooling, he is giving an irresponsible answer.

Schooling Age-In the age of schooling, when children go to school and see many things around them, their minds will generate more curiosity, so the parents need to optimize children's interests. In the schooling age, the mind grows very fast, and you should notice every child's activity once a day.

Now question which type of activity?

Like where the children are spending time more. Parents need always to take the day's report to sleep time and ask which type of problem they are facing or anything they require. Educational speech should not frequently be. If you do it, the child may be irritating. You should provide a lesson by using the Example of a famous personality.

Read conversation to know better

Conversation (8.1)

A Family has three children. We will see the schedule and how parents are dealing with them. I am dividing this conversation into two sections. The first is before school, after school, and until bedtime.

Morning time.

Father is reading the newspaper, and the mother is trying to awake the children.

Mother: Get up, kids, getting late for school.

Children: Mom, we will not go to school, want to sleep.

Mother:I want to avoid listening to any excuse. Get up soon.

Father:(Shouting on all children) get up within a second. Otherwise, I am coming there.

Children wake up and ask for tea. After that, one by one, they go to the washroom.

They are getting late for school, the bus does pass out from home, and the father picks up the children and leaves. In school, children get scolds due to late coming.

At the noon

When the children come home, they take lunch and play games. Mother is sleeping after the work of the kitchen. After 3 PM, the tuition teacher comes home and teaches to children. After completing tuition, the teacher complains to the mother about the children's homework.

Mother: Ok, sir, I'll say to his father.

Teacher: Ok

At evening

Father comes back home.

Children are playing games, and one child is doing is studying.

At the table of dinner, everyone is taking dinner.

Mother: The tuition teacher was complaining about children.

Father:started yelling, If you guys want to study, then read properly; otherwise, leave the school.

At bed Time

Father is watching TV, and the mother is going to sleep, and one child is playing a game on mobile, and one is sleeping. The third one is with the mother.

As you can see, this family is running well, and children are going to school, but parents have no plans, and they are not punctual for children. In this conversation, you can see children have no study schedule and no program of any extra activity. They are busy with useless activities. When the teacher reports children, the father is not taking the children's studies seriously. So the family has no plan.

College Age-When a child comes to college, he is more mature than earlier. But in this maturity, ego, anger, self-respect, passion will also be inside the children. This time is more valuable for every parent, do not give more speech for money, goals, and incomplete wishes. You should support them for their life goals. It would help if you did not impose your dreams on them. If your parenting is good in the initial stage and your bonding is solid with your children, they will understand your feelings and achieve your goals.

At the stage of life step, you need to guide your children, if you are not well-educated and have fewer skills for society living standard. Even then, it would be best if you encouraged your child to improve skills and try to become a hard worker. You cannot excuse that you are illiterate and cannot guide your children. You can take help from another person who can teach your child. There's nothing to be ashamed to ask for help.

After college, the career will start, and children will earn. Right earning will come from the right way, and the proper way will get from the right direction.

>>CHAPTER 9<<

THE WAY OF COMMUNICATION IS RUDE

As we know, good communication is key to a healthy relationship. When children learn the first step of communication, their parents play a vital role. So we can say parents are the first teacher of talking with children. But unknowingly, we misbehave with Childs and yell at them. This factor will maintain the communication gap between children and parents. Sometimes, if you face some issues, you become frustrated and transfer frustration to others, primarily children. This thing is not appropriate for your relation.

I am not saying that you should not shout at your children. You can but in a very light and effective way. Always yelling will kill the feelings of your child. How can you manage to yell at your child?

I'll give you some advice. Because the child is the idol of mistakes, you cannot ignore their errors. You don't need to yell at them constantly. You can control their mistakes by using many other communication styles.

For example, you are working, and your child is asking mobile phone and insisting on you, again and again, then what do you do? You have two ways: you give him or shout at him and strictly say no. But if you choose the second way, then the child will show you two types of attitude, the first thing is the child will cry loudly, and the second thing is the child will be dreary.

Now the trouble is double, whereas you can handle the situation by diverting a child's mind, or you can give something another option to the child to convince him. So, we need to understand where we have to yell at Children. With a wrong decision, we can make trouble, too.

Now let's go to some above side of life. Suppose your child wants to discuss something with you, and you are not taking any interest in listening to him. So, the child will feel helpless and feel awful. Maybe he tries to find another person outside the home to share problems. And if you are listening to the child and when the time comes to reply, you are talking very rudely or answering in a nonsense way, and the child will revoke to share things with you.

This type of nature always makes the distance between parents and children. So, always try to give a positive response softly. I can understand everywhere is the struggle in life. Everybody has a significant responsibility. But in between this, children's progression is also a considerable responsibility.

Do not abuse during the interaction with the child. If you do this, the child will learn from you and perform this outside the home, which is unsuitable for society.

Side effects of rude behavior

- **Rudeness will hurt the productivity of the child. Bad for health and wellbeing.**

- **A child can become dull.**

- **Personality Disorders.**

- **Low Self- Esteem.**

- **Acquired Behavior.**

- **Low Emotional Intelligence.**

- **Will hide problems.**

Read conversation to know better. Conversation (9.0)

Daughter: Mom, I am going to school.

Mother: Your father will drop you at school.

Father: Ready within a minute; otherwise, I'll not drop you at school.

Daughter: Yes, daddy, I am just wearing shoes.

Father: ok, quick.

The daughter and father are going on the bike.

Daughter: Daddy, What is this? (Daughter is showing for the Camel).

Father: Camel.

Daughter: What are the camels doing here?

Father: I do not know. I am not the owner of those camels (teasingly).

Daughter:I am just Asking, Daddy.

Father: Keep silence.

After Few Minutes, She makes some silent for a few minutes.

Daughter: Daddy, Today is my test.

Father: ok

Daughter: How does the train run? Daddy.

Father: I am an accountant, not a train maker. Keep silent and see straight.

Daughter: Mood Off (on the way, She is thinking why daddy is not answering me).

At Evening

Father comes to the school to pick her up.

Father: Comes Fast.

Daughter: Hello Daddy (She is happy because he is going home).

Father: No reply to Daughter.

Daughter: Daddy, Teacher, got our test today, and I got 10 out of 10 marks (Telling with Excitement).

Father: No Reply.

Daughter: How was your day, daddy?

Father: No reply.

They reached home.

Mother to Daughter

How was your school day?

Daughter: Good mom.

It is a ubiquitous conversation between children and parents. Sometimes parents do not reply to children's questions. I wouldn't say I like this behavior. The child is performing well in the above discussion, but his father behaves rudely with him. He is not responding. He is not giving a proper answer. He is not involved in the happiness of the child. If I say the father is under stress because he is not responding to the child or behaving rudely due to stress. So I'll say now he is transferring the pressure to the child.

The way of talking and communication should not always be rude, and sometimes it can be bearable but not always. You have no right to transfer your frustration to your children.

I have noticed this behavior in many parents who do not reply to their children if they ask something. Do you know this habit makes your child upset?

As we can see in the conversation, the father is not responding to test marks. If the father repeatedly does this behavior, the child will lose self-esteem.

Our rude behavior can transform into frustration. Parents' accountability to teach children at a very young age how to treat others with good manners, respect, and courtesy is one of the most important things we'll do as parents. One of the most valuable tools we can give our kids is building positive relationships with other people.

>>CHAPTER 10<<

NO HELP WHEN THEY GENUINELY NEED IT

By the way, this situation is applicable only when then your child is in an emergency. But it is also a common problem in society. As you know, in your lousy time, everyone will leave you alone to fight the issue, but sometimes parents also do that. As everybody knows, nowadays, everyone is fighting with life to succeed. So, children have a lot of pressure to take over their responsibility obligation to succeed in every stage of life. In this stage, children need support. I agree some children do not require any help, they are capable of achieving their goals themselves, but these types of children are extraordinary. In counting a hundred, only two children can fulfill their dreams without any support, and they have the skills to arrange required things to stabilize themselves. But if your child is not extraordinary, you need to support him from time to time. Every child has a different quality to live their life. You cannot compare each other. Now back to the main point. My point is to help children when they need too much. The term help has many things includes. Like that

- Support Guidance

- Money

- Health

- Trouble

- Physical challenges

- Attraction and Love

- To Build Strength

- Any legal issue

- Sex Education

The above points are necessary for normal children, so parents need to be ready to help regarding the above issues. Even though parents are unknown from the solutions, they can take guidance from others. It is also the responsibility of parents.

So, it is time to discuss the points one by one.

Support: Parents need to support their child in education and all weaknesses of body or life. I have seen somebody with two children and a physically or mentally weak child whose parents do not support or care for him. It is not good parenting. We should help the vulnerable child also and try to find out the quality of the weak child.

For Example **(Read Conversation 5.2).**

Guidance: From time to time, the direction is like a booster dose of life to make the future better for children. Sometimes parents do partiality. If one child is more intelligent and the second is less competent, then always parents give the example of the clever child to the weaker child. It would be best to support the more vulnerable child and not compare them to each other. Proper guidance will give your child the right direction, and you cannot run away from this responsibility.

For Example (Read Conversation 8.0)

Money: When the child is growing, parents should also plan for saving because this money will help career building. It may not happen that you do not have sufficient money for him starting with education. Money-saving is also needful for Child help.

For Example (Read Conversation 5.2).

Health: To maintain the child's good health, parents should help him from time to time.

Guide to children for good health, provide healthful food to them. From time to time, visit the doctor and know about children's bodies like blood group, hemoglobin, allergies, etc.

For Example (Read Conversation 5.1)

Trouble: Without any sound, the problem can come to anyone. And children are unknown about the situation. So, always understand the risk and try to know what goes wrong in the life of the children. You can decide a day to discuss with the children about their education, life, health, fitness, etc.

Read Conversation to know better.

Conversation 10.0

On holiday, the child will play in the garden with their friends. And parents are opposing him. And they said, "No, stay here at home, work with us, and share home cleaning work." Let see what's going on there.

Child:I am going outside to play with my friends.

Mother: No, stay here and help in cleaning.

Child: No, I m just coming.

Mother: no, come inside (yelling).

Child: Mom, my friends come to play with me.

The child insists on going with friends, and last he went. After some time, the child gets hurt from baseball in the garden. He falls back home with their friends.

Mother: I told you before, do not go outside. You were injured because you did not listen to me.

Child: Crying.

Mother: Go to your father, and he will treat you, do not talk to me.

Father: Why did you go there while we refused?

Child: crying.

Father is treating the child, and the mother is yelling so far. As we can see in the conversation, when the child needs parents, they show that they are older than him also show a negative attitude. They could have adopted another method not to send the child to play. They accept his obstinacy; they then impose their anger on the child. Either they should not have taken his determination or should not impose their rage on him.

Physical challenges: Physical challenges can happen to anyone, maybe for many reasons, like accidents or mishappening. So in this stage, children need extra care from the side of their parents. They require more attention and moral support from their parents. Suppose your child is studying outside the home then suddenly he sicked, I know the doctor will do everything, but as per your responsibility, you should go there and care for him. It would help if you went one step further to care for your child. Sometimes the child goes outside to study, and their meal change and the environment can make them ill to the child, then the child requires extra care from the parents. You should care for him and arrange all the necessary things for him.

For Example- A family has two children. One is disabled, and he always felt weak in writing. Always his parents give him an excuse that "You cannot be able to write."

The second child performs fine and always competes with the disabled child.

Disabled Child: I want to go for a coaching class for speaking English.

Father: No need, you can not write. Your handwriting is not good.

Child: But I can improve if I go for training.

Father: No, you will waste your time; try to understand.

It is a small conversation, but when the child needs help, his father is not helping him. Father is thinking about the weak point of the child and not trying to improve the child's confidence.

Attraction and love: I include love and attraction together because when children come at a youth age, it is natural to attach or attract and fall in someone else's love. In this stage, you should guide them and inquire about love matters.

To Build Strength: In the step of life, many challenges will come, and sometimes challenges will be extensive, and to solve them, you will need strength. And this strength will come from the parents. I am the witness of many practices. If parents are standing with the child, the child can do anything and fight with any problem. If the child wants to do something in his life, what should you do? You require to notice his dedication towards the hobby. If you find a child's dedication is genuine and wants to achieve the pursuit at any cost, you need to become his strength.

Any legal issue: In numerous instances, I noticed that all relatives suddenly leave him alone when a child comes under any legal cases or matters. Then parents also go or do not care properly, do not do this, search matter and give strength to the child. The legal issue means not criminal cases or other matters, and it also means government documentation. Sometimes other legal problems can also come. Suppose a child wants to create some valuable documents by the government-authority, you should support him, and if you have no time, you should arrange another link who can help in the legal matter.

>>CHAPTER 11<<

NOT CONSIDERING CHILDREN OPINIONS

Here I am using the term opinion because parents generally listen to the children but not their opinions. Opinion term is helpful for every parent, but how? Let's come and understand, as we know time is changing day by day with the world, generation is also changing. And when children go outside the home, like school, college, they learn many new things, which were not available in our time. Suppose In any work, if children give some idea, opinions, and suggestions, we should listen to it.

Generally, most parents give a rude reply and say, "Do not teach us. We are your parents." If you also do this, that is not good for your parenting. If you want to go ahead, you should listen to everyone surrounding you. From time to time, children's speech will change, and they will suggest to you many new things. They will recommend many things they would have seen outside the home, so you should not neglect them because children's minds are more curious than yours. Do you know an interested person can catch new things quickly? Same Like that the children will capture new stuff quickly. I am giving some examples about child opinions.

Conversation (11.0)

A father was filling a government form in front of his child, and in that form, the list of expenses given in Hindi alphabets, suddenly the child comes and asks the father, what are you doing daddy.

Daddy: Do your work. I am doing my urgent work, do not disturb me.

Child: Silent, Continuously watching daddy.

Daddy: Don't go over my head. Take your chair.

Suddenly, the child notices daddy making a mistake in making the serial. The child says (with a slow sound) Daddy, after the थ, द will come. Daddy sees this mistake and corrects it quickly.

Daddy: Does not reply to child and does not give any appreciation to the child.

Dady is doing their work. The child goes inside the room and playing. So what do you think by this example? Father should respond to the child and appreciate his work if you are doing something that is not good for your existence in the child's eye. Like this, many examples are in society.

Do you know the child is greedy for appreciation? If you appreciate him for his excellence, his motivation will boost. He will do more excellent work in society. Do you know the child has a small world in their mind? And in this world, many things rotate frequently. The second truth of the life of children is parents happiness. So they will do everything to make you happy, but in the tiny mind of children not have good sense.

Due to this vague sense, we need to understand the child's little mind.

Second Conversation (11.1)

A family has two children, and the father works in the private sector, and the mother is a housewife. Father wants to purchase an Electronic Item to use for office work. Then, the father discussed with colleagues the brand name of the item. Colleagues of the father are old generation and have no good knowledge of technology. So let see what's happening. At night at the table, Dinner time.

Father:I want to purchase a laptop for my office work.

Children:(Unknown XYZ) company laptop is good. It has a high configuration and good battery backup with the latest technology system.

One child: My friend's father purchased this laptop a year ago, it is working fine.

Second Child: My teacher also uses this laptop. It has a high configuration.

Father: Ok, let see. I'll ask others tomorrow as well.

Next-Day Office

Father Talking with Colleagues.

My children said, "Unknown XYZ company's laptop is good and working fine." Also, they are saying, have good technical parts and machinery.

Colleague: Where are you paying attention to the things of the children? They do not know about the value of money, this type of Laptop would be costly. At the same price, we will take another one and save money.

Colleague: Buy the Laptop of the Company (Unknown ABC). It was good.

Father: I think you are right. So, what do I do?

Colleague: You can purchase a Laptop from this company.

Father: did you use this Laptop.

Colleagues: No, but do not worry, I know about it.

Same Day: At the dining table.

Father: I have decided on Laptop (Unknown ABCD).

Children: But daddy, this Laptop is hard to run and lower configuration, and it is not for you. These laptops are helpful for learning purposes and are very costly laptops for lower configuration. If you add more, you can buy a high configuration Laptop.

Father: No, my colleagues referred me Unknown ABCD company Laptop. It is at the best price.

Father: Ok, make your Dinner, you are children do not speak more between elders.

Children are Silently Eating.

At bedtime

Children are talking to each other. Why is daddy wasting money on that Laptop? Daddy should listen to us. My teacher is also using this.

I also used this Laptop in my school library. It was a lower configuration and also a slow laptop.

Next Day

Father purchased the Laptop, which the Colleagues suggested.

On Dining Table.

Father: Laptop looking good but too much costly this month budget was disturbed.

My children said, "Unknown XYZ company's laptop is good and working fine." Also, they are saying, have good technical parts and machinery.

Colleague: Where are you paying attention to the things of the children? They do not know about the value of money, this type of Laptop would be costly. At the same price, we will take another one and save money.

Colleague: Buy the Laptop of the Company (Unknown ABC). It was good.

Father: I think you are right. So, what do I do?

Colleague: You can purchase a Laptop from this company.

Father: did you use this Laptop.

Colleagues: No, but do not worry, I know about it.

Same Day- At the dining table.

Father: I have decided on Laptop (Unknown ABCD).

Children: But daddy, this Laptop is hard to run and lower configuration, and it is not for you. These laptops are helpful for learning purposes and are very costly laptops for lower configuration. If you add more, you can buy a high configuration Laptop.

Father: No, my colleagues referred me Unknown ABCD company Laptop. It is at the best price.

Father: Ok, make your Dinner, you are children do not speak more between elders.

Children are Silently Eating.

At bedtime

Children are talking to each other. Why is daddy wasting money on that Laptop? Daddy should listen to us. My teacher is also using this.

I also used this Laptop in my school library. It was a lower configuration and also a slow laptop.

Next Day

Father purchased the Laptop, which the Colleagues suggested.

On Dining Table.

Father: Laptop looking good but too much costly this month budget was disturbed.

Children: Yes, Daddy, Laptop is costly.

Next Day

Father is going to the office and taking the Laptop as well. When he reached the office In the office, Colleagues gave congratulation to the father. Father started working on Laptop

After few days

Father is saying to Colleagues. This Laptop is hanging again and again.

Colleague: You are taking too much work from this Laptop, that's why it is going to hang. Yes, Daddy, Laptop is costly.

Father: But I am doing routine work on it.

Same Day Evening at Dining Table.

Father: Laptop is going hang. Can anyone help?

One Child: Daddy, you are using high graphics software programs.

Father: So this Laptop will not support?

Children: This Laptop has less configuration, daddy.

Father: I will exchange my Laptop.

Everyone is eating silently.

In this conversation, children give opinions on the Laptop with confidence because they watch the technology surrounding them. In their college, Laptop and the latest technology is in use, that's why they are suggesting to their father. But the father is not listing and not searching for opinions of children. And Father is also known that there are very few technical skills in their office. After that, he neglects the idea of children.

>>CHAPTER 12<<

SHOWING TOO MUCH CARE AND PAMPERING

Too much care love is like the slowest form of weakness. And too much care is like the form of poison. Yes, you read precisely right. Too much love and care will make your child weak and loose. Too much love and care work like a soother. Without it, a child cannot be calm. When a child cries frequently, then we give soother inside his mouth, then the child sucks it and becomes tranquil, but without the soother, the child cannot become tranquil. That's why too much care and pampering is not suitable for children. It does addict like a soother.

It would help if you cared for your children until you were alive. It is the parent's dharma (responsibility) to care for children. If you care for your children by heart, your child will also care for you. As I told you before, children are the mirror of your karma. Maybe some parents say our children do not care about us, and they are busy in their lives and are not spending time with us. So, in this case, you will have to build a foundation initially to obtain care from your children. Why does too much pampering will make your child weak?

I am not saying that you should not love your children, but remember your limit. Anything which is crossing the boundary is harmful. Like that, excessive love and care make children addicted to it. Once the children become addicted, they will repeatedly ask for the same things. How is excessive pampering not good for your child?

Suppose your child's age is three years old, and he is understanding pampering, and you are doing everything like feeding, changing clothes, convincing for anything, etc. Now, what will happen? Your child will expect this from everyone that they will love and care for him.

If this love doesn't have isn't gotten from someone else, the child will feel helpless. The nature of the child will be jumpy. If your care and love are not excessive, then he'll try to adjust. It is an example of a small child. Suppose your child's age is in years or more when he will go to school and there he found something missing like food, environment, friend or others.

Then definitely, he will try to skip school because he is addicted to your pampering and care and facility.

In his mind, pampering will rotate. He will think about your care and pampering because he is addicted. If the school canteen has good food and nobody is present to serve because there is self-service, the child will hesitate, and his mind will divert again towards the home facility. He will feel uncomfortable, and in between, some other children laugh at him, then the situation will become complicated.

So, how can we control excessive pampering and care? I believe that with love and care, some boldness is also necessary. And how this boldness will come, this boldness will come from your bold nature. Your children are your strength, and you are the strength of your children. Every parent should make their child bold. After that, your child becomes your power. Now come to the point, how can we control pampering? I am giving some bullet points that can help you. Let see the conversation to know better.

Conversation (12.0)

A family has a daughter and one son (Sam). Parents care child too much, always care about education, health, and fitness. Most of the time, parents give focus on their daughter. Parents think their daughter (Jerry) is brittle and needs more care and love.

Let's see what's going on.

Morning time

Mother: Jerry, wake up and take your bed- tea.

Jerry: Yes, Mom.

Mother: Jerry, Come and hug me. I love you so much, my princes. (Jerry Hugs to mother).

Mother: Take your toothbrush and do paste fast.

After that, take a bath, and I am preparing your breakfast. What would you want to take?

Jerry: Mom, I'll take egg and bread omelet only.

Mother: Ok, I am preparing, my Dear.

On Dining Table

Father: How are you, Jerry?

Jerry:I am fine, daddy.

Jerry: Daddy, I do not want to go by school bus.

Father: No problem, Dear, I'll drop you.

Son: But Daddy, I'll go on the school bus.

Father: Ok

At evening Time

Mother: Jerry, How's your study going on? And your Sam?

Sam: Mom, the teacher gave the note to Jerry for math, and I got good marks in math.

Mother: What happened, Jerry?

Jerry: Mom teacher is not teaching me correctly. She is such a dull teacher.

Father: Ok, no concern, I'll talk to your principal.

Next Day

Morning time

Jerry: Mom, I am not feeling well today, and I do not want to go to school.

Sam: Mom, but I'll go because today's is our class test. Jerry, you should also go.

Mother: Do not force Jerry. She is not feeling well.

At noon

Jerry: Mom, I want to eat pizza.

Mother:I'll call for you, do not worry, my Dear.

Jerry is taking pizza and watching TV, and now she is not looking ill at all.

Father is calling to mother, again and again, to ask about her health.

Father is worried for Jerry, and Mother is also taking care of her.

Father: How's the Jerry?

Mother: She is taking a rest, I called the doctor, and he said everything is fit and fine.

Father: Thank God everything is Fine.

At evening time

Sam: Mom, the teacher gave me a monthly report card of Jerry. Would you please sign on it?

Mother: Jerry gets zero marks in two subjects. It is too bad.

Father: We will change the school, this school is not suitable for our daughter.

Jerry: Thanks, Daddy.

Next Day, Sunday

The mother cleans the house, the father reads the newspaper, and Jerry watches TV. Sam is playing cricket with their friends in the garden.

Jerry: Mom, I want water.

Mother: Just a minute, dear, I am coming.

Jerry: Come fast, Mom, I am thirsty too much.

Mother left the work, and she gave water to Jerry.

Jerry: Mom, I have some dirty clothes as well.

Mother: Do not worry, dear, I'll wash it soon.

Jerry: Daddy, I'll go shopping. I want some money.

Father: Do not worry. When you go, then I'll give you.

As you can see in the conversation, parents provide the girl with too much care and pampering. Due to this, the girl will begin to be lazy. She is running away from the study because her parents are not taking care of her result. They are making a big mistake here.

How can we make our children strong?

I am giving some points to make your child strong and improve behavior.

Sleep separately from your child.

Slightly shift your child into a separate room to sleep. One and two days or a maximum of 15 days child will have trouble sleeping separately from you, but once he understands, you will feel he is becoming bold in lifestyle. But remember that he should not think that you are doing this intentionally. If a child feels this, he will spy many things about you and try to know why you are doing this? Child mind will try to spy on you.

Build the habit of self-service.

This habit plays a vital role in everyone's life. If children learn this habit at the initial age, they will be addicted to self-service. Now, how can we fill up this inside your child's mind? You can share admire of our saints or legends in front of children. Children would be inspired and adopt this habit immediately. Self-service includes many things.

- Dress washing food serving.

- Setup of own room.

- Care of health.

- Care of cleaning.

It is the responsibility of parents to teach how to manage things related to self-service? When your child becomes elder, he will not have to face issues in their daily routine. And when children notice that this manner is not present in other children studying with your children, and then your children will feel proud. Children will feel something different when they get appreciation from teachers and seniors.

>>CHAPTER 13<<

NOT SHOWING ANY CARE & LOVE

Now come to the essential point of this book, parents do not show any care and love towards their children. I saw many parents who did not care for their children. Parents are busy in their life and fighting with life issues. Children of such parents feel alone and misguided in every field. Their confidence level will down always. They will hesitate to share their views with anyone. We have read in the above chapter about "Too much care and love," but this chapter is more important than the above chapter. Too much care is usual for parents, but parents are not showing any love and care; that is an exceptional case.

I am explaining some parents' behavior for children.

Less care, when the children are growing up

I saw at many places; parents give less care and love to their children after they grow up. Some parents think their children are mature and do not need supervision and love. But it is a wrong perception, and children always want care and love from parents. It is not necessary to show respect, and it is your responsibility. Your care will make your children strong and confident.

You should be aware of every activity of your children, and then you will become a good caretaker. To know better, read the conversation.

(Conversation No. 13.0)

A family has two children and both sons. Both have passed intermediate and preparing for competitive examinations.

Son: Daddy, we go outside the city to purchase some books.

Father: Ok, you can go.

Mother: Now both of you are young. Can make your decision yourself.

Father: Yes, no need to ask little things from us.

Son: We will come back late at night, mom.

Mother: How much?

Son: Approximately 2 AM night.

Father: Mother: Ok, go.

They came back late at night. And on the way, one son's lost their mobile on the highway.

Next Day

Son: Daddy, I want new mobile.

Father: Why?

Son: I have lost my mobile last night.

Mother: Oh my god, maybe the phone was stolen.

Son: Maybe.

Father: You should not have come back late at home.

Son: Yes, obviously, you permitted us last day, daddy.

Mother: We were thinking you both of them are mature.

Father: Ooufff So sad.

Mother: Our Mistake.

Parents show less care and think their children have been more mature. But in actual practice, it is not valid. Parents cannot be careless about children. Parents should have to stop the child from coming home late at night.

Parents are not interested in children.

Such parents are rare, and they do not have any interest in children. But I saw that parents are busy with their growth but not concerned about children's growth in many cases. It is simple logic that if you show interest in children, they will pay attention to you, otherwise be ready to be alone in the future. Some undeveloped or immature parents experience their children as an unwanted, intimidating dependency load. Now, the main point is that why parents make this mistake?

I am giving some reasons to you that will help you understand better.

The Depressed Parents.

Depressed parents have a mental health condition or Mental disorder. They face mental problems in their life. The emotional limit of that type of parent is limited. If they get any scary news, then they become unhappy. It is also a big reason why parents do not love their children. If any child grows up with a depressed parent, it is like growing with a ghost. The mind and mood of this type of parent will change frequently. That's why I am saying it is like increasing with wraiths.

Depression is a terrific illness, but it can be curable. If you or someone you know suffers from depression, you should not ignore it and go to the doctor for treatment. By this action, you will save the lives of many children and will secure many families.

The Aggressive Parents

In the starting, a person will anger and become aggressive after a few minutes. It is also a symptom of mental illness or weakness. This type of parent never cares where they are standing and stays ready to shout at their children. I'll put these parents in line with disturbed parents.

Parents who give Silent Treatment

The silent treatment is also part of angry parents, but the mode of treatment is changed. It can be typical to talk to someone when angry, but shutting out children with silent treatment is very damaging and immature. The children will be depressed. His mind will influence of Inferiority complex. So if you are angry with your child, you should not stop the talk. Tackle your anger with smartness. The silent treatment will transfer from one person to another, and miscommunication will create when nobody talks to each other.

We can see how parents give the silent treatment to children in this conversation.

(Conversation 13.1)

This conversation is between mother and son, and the son is ten years old. Son came from school and asked for Food. He is too much hungry.

Son: Mom, I want to eat Dal rice.

Mother: No, I cooked pumpkin.

Son: I'm not too fond of this food, you know very well, mom.

Mother: Pumpkin is good for health.

Son: I am Hungry, give me fast.

Mother: If you want to eat, then eat, otherwise arrange yourself.

Mother: I'll give you tomato sauce with it.

Son: Mom, make Dal rice, please!

Mother: No, I am not gratis for you. Take this food, your father, and I also take this food; you are not unique.

Son: Ok, Silent (Seating on the table).

Mother: Take and eat.

After one bite, the son leaves the plate of food. He went to the room. Food is on the table as it is.

After some time

Mother yells to son, why did you not finish your food?

Son: I wouldn't say I like this food (Tone- angry).

Mother: You are wasting food. I will complain to your father.

Son: Why did you not cook Dal rice for me?

Mother: One, you're wasting food and even making arguments with me.

Son: (Eating chips and ignoring to mother).

In anger, the mother goes away from there.

At Evening

Mother is cooking in Kitchen and father is watching TV and son comes in Kitchen.

Son: What are you cooking, mom.

Mom: (No Reply).

Son: Mom, are you hear me?

Mom: No reply.

Son: Tomorrow is my sports day. I'll play on the basketball team.

Mother: No reply.

Son went away from there.

Next Day

Mother is preparing the food in the Kitchen, and the son is getting ready for school.

The mother silently put the son's lunch box on the table and said nothing.

Son: ok Mom, I am going bye-bye.

Mother: No Reply, and turned towards the room.

Son: Feeling Sad.

In this conversation, we can see the mother is trying to give the silent treatment to the son. When Son asks for the Dal rice and the mother refuses the son's demand, the Son remains hungry. In this conversation, two types of options are available to understand.

First: Mother should know before that her son will not eat the pumpkin. So she should arrange anything alternative for him. The mother should set another option for the son.

Second: If the mother cannot complete the demand, and the son is to leave the food plate, she should not have to use the silent treatment.

Suppose matured people do this, then how children will understand human behavior. The silent treatment is very harmful to children. It will generate depression in the tiny mind of children. They may feel insecure and have a mental illness caused in children. Otherwise, children will be jittery and will disrespect their parents. No matter what happens, do not stop the conversation.

Parents Who Make Toxic "Jokes" on Children

Every child has some flaws, but some parents make toxic jokes about children's weaknesses. That is not fair in any way. Suppose a child is taller, then parents will make a joke on him, or the child is minor, then make a joke on him. This type of behavior shows parents do not care about the child and his feelings.

To know better, read the conversation.

A family has two children, a girl, and a boy. The boy is a fatty and dark complexion, and the girl is fair and beautiful. Invariably, the parents make toxic jokes about the boy in fun.

In the Morning

Father: Wake up, fatty boy, clean your face to become fairer.

Mother: Nobody is like this in our family.

At evening

Father: Hey, Fatty boy, give me my Specs, please.

Son to his sister: Did you see my book?

Sister: No, find out yourself.

Son: Please find I could not see here.

Sister: You need more light; after that, you will see.

Son: you mean I cannot see?

Sister: Black color requires more light to shine.

After this, both fight with each other.

In this conversation, why are parents making toxic jokes on children? They are trying to tease the children, or they do not like their children. Sometimes to take revenge on the children, parents make jokes at them because children were not listening to him.

If parents make toxic jokes on children, children will lose self-confidence between peoples. They can hate you.

They fail to provide you with support and Security.

Parents fail to provide you the Security and support, which means they do not care about you. Suppose somebody is teasing the child in school or society and the child is complaining to the parents and parents are not taking this matter seriously, it means they do not care about you. If they love you, then he will care about you.

If you are a child and reading this chapter, what should you do? Do you know this is not your fault and that your parent does not care about you? It is your parent's problem, but you bear it because you do not know how to come out of this. I am giving some bullet points to come out from this problem.

- **Do your work and focus on your life.**

- **Always keep the arrangement of emergency things which is you require.**

- **Take a backup of money consistently.**

- **Keep updated and do your study well.**

- **Make your good friend circle**

- **Keep in touch with your relative always.**

- **Learn new skills that will always help you to earn.**

- **Show Affection in Public to your parents.**

- **Celebrate happiness with him.**

If you are a parent and reading this chapter, how can you control your mistake? To solve this problem, first, you should know about the root. To find out why you are not loving and caring to your children after that, find out the solution. If you are in depression, take care of it.

- Remove misunderstanding between you and the children.

- Do not expect more from children.

- The partner should remove misunderstandings.

- Remove the ego of money from your mind. Your real wealth is your children.

- Think your child come on the earth based on you, and you will do like this, so where he will go.

- Try to know the quality of your children. They will have something different.

>>CHAPTER 14<<

NOT READY TO UPDATE WITH CHILDREN

It is also a big mistake of most parents. They do not want to upgrade with their children. Suppose a young boy lives abroad and the culture is different from the native country of his parents. And when he calls his parents to visit overseas, their parents excuse that they can not come to visit. The reason may be they are not familiar with the overseas culture. Do you know most children have a quality that they want to share every happiness with their parents? And if parents avoid it, the child feels alone. Otherwise, the child will search for another person to share. Here the value of parents will go down day by day, and child will ignore their parents in every decision of their life.

It is also possible that parents do not want to adopt the latest generation, Always they want to follow old technology. I think parents should update with the time. If they do not do it, they will feel distance from children and time. And that is called the generation gap, and it is a big problem in society. If you are not ready to upgrade, you will face many issues with your relatives and children. So how can you be prepared for your new generation? The generation gap can cause misunderstanding between the children and parents.

I believe in keeping learning. I am giving some bullet points that will help you.

Do not think that you can not learn new things.

Most of the old parents think that they can not learn new things. That is not good thinking, no age limit for learning new things. If you update yourself, you will get standardization in the vision of society. In the initial stage, I understand that you will feel uncomfortable. And Youngers will avoid you to teach. But with the help of your soft corner of heart, you will achieve the youngster's support. When you treat as a seeker, you will get knowledge as a mentor.

(Conversation 14.0)

A family has a son and old parents, and the son lives with the family. Parents are searching for a bride for their son. Son does not have more time for his parents. He is always busy with their office projects. Let see what's happening.

Father: Dear son, Pandit Ji suggests a girl for you if you have time to fix a meeting with her family.

Son: Daddy, I do not have sufficient time for that work. You both can decide what is better for me?

Mother: But, Dear son, we should know her very well about the question of life.

Son: Ok, I manage the time for this work.

Next Day

Son: Mom, I have decided we can go on Sunday to see the girl.

Father: That is great

Sunday

Families are talking to each other, and the son asks some questions to the girl, he does not get a good answer from her. Also, girl family does not like the work of boy. Both families decide to do not to go ahead in relation.

After a Few Days.

Mother: Dear Son, Pandit Ji suggests a new girl for you.

Son: Mom, I have no time for this, last time already I have wasted my time too.

Father: But we will have to take any decision.

Son: Daddy, please try to understand. I have no time. I have a lot of work for my office project.

Father: So what do we do now?

Son: You can use another option, daddy. Download any matrimony application on mobile or visit the website, there you can choose the perfect girl, and then we will discuss it with her online. After that, we will go to meet her family.

Father: Oh, We do not know the application and online system.

Son: Try to do. I will teach you, daddy.

Mother: At this age, that is not possible.

Father:we can not learn, and we do not want to know.

Mother: Yes, Pandit Ji will give us details, and we will call him.

Son: Matrimony website is a good option, a time-saving option, Daddy.

Father: We can not do it.

Son: Ok, do as you want to do.

It is a nominal conversation, and it shows many things. It offers a misunderstanding of the generation gap. It shows that the parents do not want to update, even the son is ready to teach them. I also consider this is a mistake; learning or not wanting to learn is different. At least they should try. I believe there is no age to learn; They can get knowledge at any stage of life. In this conversation, parents are not illiterate but unwilling to upgrade to the latest technology. If they tried to upgrade, and suppose they got failure, they can tell the son that they tried for this option.

Do not be shy to ask anything.

It is an important point, and if you shy to learn new things, you cannot achieve anything. Don't be hesitating to ask anything. Hesitation works as a breaker to obtain knowledge. Suppose parents are coming from a village and going to a shopping mall with their children and children are lives in the city already, and parents see the escalator in the mall, and they are not aware of how to use it. Then they will avoid the escalator and give an excuse to children that they will use manual stairs. However, they could ask for help from children if they wanted.

(Conversation 14.1)

A family has two children, and both children are working in an MNC company. Parents are retired, and most of the time does spend at home. They meet their children in the evening time only. They are thinking of an E-commerce business online from home.

Father and Mother: Dear Son, we're thinking of some work from home.

Son: Sure, if you want to do, you can do.

Mother: ok

Son: If you need anything, can ask me anytime.

Next Day

They are searching for many online websites and their prospects.

Mother: We will ask son, do not take stress (To husband).

Father: No, no need, what he will think about us.

Father: He will think that his parents are illiterate.

Mother: Ok, we can find someone others for this.

Try to communicate with your children on the latest news.

If you listen to the latest news and do not know about it, you should always discuss it. If nobody has time to give you the information, you should wait for this news again. This habit makes you up to date consistently in the home and society.

>>CHAPTER 15<<

DO NOT MAKE YOUR CHILDREN WEAK

Weakness is the slowest form of failure. Weak children or people can not achieve anything in their life, because they can not step ahead. Most parents make their children soft because they have insecurity in their minds. I am giving some common mistakes that make your children weak.

Are you maximizing common fear of children?

Most parents maximize the common fear of children, and they will expand the slight fear into a considerable dread and add some lies. For example, a child gets scared of a lizard, and his parents will use this fear to control the child. The parent will say, "Lizard bite will make your body swell." His bite will kill you, his poison will make you mad, and here parents are adding some extra lies also. This fear will take home inside the children's minds. They should tell the genuine reason to the child. Let see the conversation to know better.

(Conversation 15.0)

The son is going with his mother on the road; suddenly, he sees the cat crossing them. Son asks mother, mom, the cat looks different and seems dangerous. Mom, yes, he crossed our way, so we should wait.

Son: Why, mom?

Mother: Ancestors say if a cat crossed our way, we should stop and wait for some time.

Son: If we do not do so?

Mother: Maybe something terrible will happen.

Son: Something terrible, like?

Mother: I do not know correctly, but I think death in an accident.

Son: (Getting scared in his mind, this fear making space).

After Few Minutes.

Son: Mom, Cat, will do the accident?

Mother: Maybe.

Son: oh

Mother: Cat has sharp nails. It can scratch anyone with nails.

Mother: If the cat scratches your face, marks will show on your face.

Son: Oh, dangerous.

Mother: Cat picks up small children who do not listen to their parents.

Son: Cat can harm me also?

Mother: Yes, of course.

Mother: If you obey your elders, the cat will spare you.

Next Day

The mother calls their son for dinner, and the son is busy watching TV.

Mother: Dear son, Come and take your dinner.

Son: I am watching my cartoon, will take dinner later.

Mother: Switch off the TV, dear.

Son: You eat, mom.

Mother: ok, as you wish.

Mother is saying to father.

Sam, do you know? Last night, a cat had entered our house. Sam (loudly) yes, I saw, she is searching for something, I think.

Son: (suddenly comes in the kitchen) Mom, I am fearing.

Mother: Ok, take your dinner fast. The cat will spare you.

Son: Yes, I am obeying you.

Son is taking dinner in panic, and his parents are laughing silently. They think they have won. Many questions rotate in the son's mind and make him in trouble. This fear will set in the son's mind, and if parents take advantage of this fear, again and again, this fear will maximize in the child's mind.

Let Failure Happen

Without failure, you can not succeed. Some parents are scared of failure, and they also teach it to their children. Children get benefit from experiencing loss. We know this, and it's hard to accept for adults. Many parents equate good parenting with preventing their kids from struggling. If children fail, do not tell them to skip the task step. Encourage him to attempt the task again. If you encourage him to try the job again, they will learn many new things.

Sometimes I see parents refuse to children to try new things. They're afraid that something will happen wrong. Suppose a child wants to play a cycle, then parents will take it very seriously and say you are small for this when you become mature, then you can use it. For examples

The matchbox

For example, a child is trying to use the match, and Parents are saying, "keep away from the matchbox. It is dangerous". We should teach the child appropriately for this action, like its use, safety precautions, etc. If we spread the fear about the matchbox, the child will learn this activity very late. This type of small cleverness will make your child smarter.

Reading Time Watch

When children try to learn to clock, then parents do not take an interest and say when you become mature, you will know automatically, this is not fair you should try with the child.

Note- We should teach everything in our presence.

Cycling

The child will be excited to learn to Cycle, and if parents say no due to being afraid of injury, the child will never know the cycling. He will often fall and may be injured, but if he tries, again and again, he will be able to cycle one day.

Show to Your Child that How to Face Fears?

Suppose your child is afraid of the dark or terrified to meet new people, then you should help your child face their fears. If your child avoids anything scary, they'll never gain the confidence.

Read conversation to know better.

(Conversation 15.1).

The family is watching a horror movie with a child, suddenly the horror scene comes, and the child becomes scared. After watching the film, the child is worried, and he feels like someone is behind the door. Then his mother teaches him how to face the fear and a lesson for a lifetime.

Mother: What happened, dear son?

Son: Mom, Something is hiding behind the gate.

Mother: No, Dear, it is an illusion of the mind.

Son: In the movie, a ghost comes from the gate.

Mother: It's just a movie, only for entertainment purposes.

Son: No, I'll not go towards the room gate.

Mother: Ok, I'll go with you, and we will remove your fear together.

Son: Ok, but you go ahead.

Mother: Ok, come and see, nothing is here.

Mother: Look, dear son, when we see any horror seen in the movie, our unconscious mind imagines this horror surrounding us, but in actual practice, it is not absolute.

Son: So it is just an illusion.

Mother: Yes.

Mother: If you watch a comedy movie, you will feel happy. And your mind becomes fresh and naughty.

Son: Yes, mom.

Son:I understand now. I'll not be scared.

In the above conversation, we can see how the mother shows how we can face fear because she is telling the actual truth to the son. This positive guidance will always help the son, and he will never be scared from horror movies.

Now the question is that, how can you help?

- Do not maximize the fear.

- Explain the truth of fear.

- Find out the reason for anxiety and then explain to the child.

- Do not avoid facing the fear.

- Stand with your child to face the fear.

- Give the confidence to fight with fear.

- Do not spread rumors.

- Treat with specific skills.

You should teach consistency to your kids also to do better next time, not making them suffer for mistakes. Use consequences that teach specific skills, such as problem-solving skills, impulse control, and self-discipline. These skills will help your child to behave. This skill will generate self-confidence inside the children's minds.

Let Your Child Make Mistakes

Mistake teaches many things to everyone. Teach your children that mistakes are part of the learning process. So they will not feel ashamed or harassed about getting something wrong. It is the responsibility of parents to teach the lesson of learning from mistakes.

Allow Your Child to struggle.

As you know, without hard work, we can not achieve happiness. Struggles will help your child to build mental power. If they face a battle in the initial stage of life, they will learn many things by experience. So, let your child lose allow them to feel bored. During the drudgery time, they will learn many fundamentals of life. Your children will lose their life weaknesses by this step, and we will also appreciate this.

Allow your child to make the decision.

This point is also critical because most parents do not allow their children to make any decisions. They think that their children are minor in age. If you do this, your children do not learn new things in their lives. They will depend upon you, and a time you will come to irritate from your children. And you may say, "You are useless. Look at the other children, and they are experts in all."

Are you constantly expecting perfection?

High expectations are suitable for kids. The expectation from your children is reasonable because this expectation gives a path to your children. It also works like a backfire to motivate your child. But if you are always expecting, then that is not good. Whether you expect too much from your child on the sports field or your academic expectations are unreasonable, kids who feel they can't succeed are likely to stop trying.

But this expectation turns into depression when you always expect perfection. It is not compulsory that consistently achieve perfection.

If you always expect perfection from your children and fail to achieve perfection, they will be away from your given task. And somewhere, this will take the turn into the weakness.

Do not ignore the slight fear of children.

Sometimes parents do not care about the slight fear of the children. They will have to care for these types of worries. Suppose a child is scared with a horror character or a personality, ignoring this fear, then this fear will become a weakness of mind. These small fears will turn into big fear. The small worries become paramount in the life of children. If parents face it with the dare, they will learn to face fears.

Common fears in children

- Fear from Darkness.

- Divorce of their parents

- Supernatural Fears

- Death

- Separation

There are many factors of Child fearing.

Genetic susceptibility – some children are generally more sensitive and emotional in their temperament.

At least one anxious parent-children learn how to behave from watching their parents.

Overprotective parenting – a dependent child is more likely to feel helpless, leading to generalized anxiety.

Due to some Bad and stressful events – Like parental separation, an injury, or hospital stay.

Due to some Bad and stressful events– Like parental separation, an injury, or hospital stay.

>>CHAPTER 16<<

IMPOSING YOUR GOALS ON YOUR KIDS

Every person has their goals in life. For some people, this goal does complete, and for some not. Then they will try to find out their own goals in their children's future.

How do parents project their goals onto their children? I am giving a case study to know better.

A father is a reputed government officer, he wanted to become an admin officer, but currently, he is working for a formal job in the government sector. But he could not become an admin officer due to the lower percentage in graduation. On that day, he thought that a good percentile was only the way to get a promising career or job. After marriage, he decided to make his children an admin officer to fulfill his dream.

Now see the conversation of that father with his children.

Conversation (16.0)

Father: Hey, son, you are in 10th standard.

Son: Yes Daddy.

Father: You will have to get a good percentage in the exam.

Son: Yes, dad, I'll try my best (Genuine answer).

Father: No, I do not want to listen to anything. I want a good percentage; you will have to become an admin officer.

Son: I will try my best (with uncomfortable tone).

Father: I do not want to listen to the word 'try.' I want results. (Angry tone).

Son: Daddy, I want some new musical equipment to learn.

Father: No, focus on studying. You can do everything you want after becoming an admin officer in the government.

Son: but Daddy.

Father: no, go inside and do study.

Son: Ok, daddy.

You can see this; it is a very nominal conversation in every family. But if you notice, the son is under the pressure of his father's dream. And the father is killing the dreams of the son. It is called projecting/imposing goals on children.

Come and learn the positive way of projecting a goal. There is no guarantee that your dream will come true in both methods. But in the above scenario, children will face mental pressure that is not good for child health. Otherwise, the child will suffer from depression and feel uncomfortable. And you know very well in the depression, nobody can achieve anything.

Now, what is the positive way to project a goal?

Father: Dear son, congrats, you are in 10th standard. Do you know? When I was in graduation, I could not achieve a good percentage for some reason, so I could not become an admin officer. If you get good marks on the exam, I'll feel complete.

Son: Yes, daddy, I'll try my best.

Father: Son, if you want anything required, you can ask me.

Son: Yes, daddy, I want a musical instrument to learn.

Father: Yes, dear son, you can buy this instrument to learn. But on one condition, you will not lose your study due to this requirement. And you will fix a time to learn this instrument.

Son: Yes, as you say, daddy.

In the above conversation, we can see the method of communication with children. The second conversation between child and father is very smooth, and the child is very comfortable with his father sharing views.

Only career goal projection is not on my list. I am giving some more examples where we project goals on children.

Let see the conversation (16.1)

Mom: Dear daughter, come to the kitchen and take your soup, which is healthy for your health.

The daughter comes into the kitchen

Daughter: Which soup did you make, mom?

Mom:I made the soup of Bitter gourd.

Daughter: I wouldn't say I like this soup.

Mom: I take this soup daily to maintain my weight and body. It would help if you took this also.

Daughter: No, mom, I do not need it. I am fit and fine.

Mom: You will have to make this soup. It is my order to you.

Daughter: No, mom, I want some solid food in the morning. I am feeling hungry.

Daughter: Mom, I like the tomato soup.

Mom: No, you will take only the Bitter gourd soup.

Daughter: Run away from the kitchen and cry.

In this conversation, we can see, mom is forcing the daughter to take the soup.

The mother is not telling any benefits to the child, and she is just forcing her to take the soup. Many parents project their goals like the above conversation.

Positive way to talk with children

In this case, how to do positive talk with children.

Mom: Dear daughter, come to the kitchen. I am making something healthy for us.

Daughter: Yes, Mom, I am coming (Excited).

Daughter: What are you cooking, mom.

Mom: Dear baby, do you know about the Bitter gourd, it is a very healthy food, which controls sugar and it has more benefits. But it has some bitter taste, but do not worry, I am adding something new ingredients in the soup to make it tasty.

Daughter: I do not like this Soup mom, I like only tomato soup.

Mom: My dear daughter, you can sip a bit of this soup for health; after that, I'll make tomato soup for you.

Daughter:ok, I'll try.

The daughter becomes convinced to sip a Bitter gourd's soup in this conversation.

If the daughter is ready to take a sip of this soup, it means your task will be complete. May be daughter likes the taste, and she will demand this soup again. Suppose your daughter rejects your offer and gives you the wrong answer, "I can not sip this soup," so you should not force her if she does not require it.

In the above conversation, we can see how parents impose their goals on children.

Parents are not aware that they are making mistakes; they think they are doing good for their children. Knowingly or unknowingly, they are making mistakes.

In this conversation, we should think the daughter has no requirement for Bitter gourd soup because she is fit, but the mother requires bitter gourd soup. The mother assumes that the daughter also needs soup, but she does not need it. So I can say the mother is conscious of their daughter, but she is imposing her Possessiveness on the daughter.

Many parents impose their goals on children, but this is not fair. I am not saying that you should not give goals to your children, but you should not impose your dreams on children.

It would help if you taught your child to high thinking to achieve success. If children think high, they will be able to generate their own goals, and maybe these goals are better than your goals.

>>CHAPTER 17<<

NO ENCOURAGEMENT FOR HIGH THINKING

If your thinking is high, you can achieve many things in your life because high thought makes your personality bold. Without any consideration, you can not achieve anything. If you think heightened, you will try to learn heightened, and if you know heightened, your mind will expand.

Many peoples I saw in my life whose thinking level is minimal. They do not want to gain more. My meaning for gain is not about money. I intend to achieve high standards and skills in society.

If parents think high, then children definitely will think high. Many parents say, "What we have to do, we have just to eat Dal Roti" It means parents are not interested in doing something new in their life. They are investing their energy in passing life. This message will go to the children, and they will also think very little, and if their thinking level is minor, they can not achieve a better life.

The meaning of high thinking is not related to the technical terminology; high thinking means great thoughts like our legends. High thinking makes you a legend personality, and high thinking has two ways to adopt. One is a good book; the second is a good society. Good books and a good community gives motivation and direction to life also.

Now back to our topic, how parents are making mistakes to not sharing high thoughts. I am giving some conversation for better understanding.

The conversation first (17.0)

A relative comes home. Parents are doing general discussions with relatives about the children. Relative is speaking the exemplary achievements of their children to the parents. Parents are listening and praised for their work. Suddenly, the parent's child comes into the room and wishes to the relative. Let see.

Relative: How are you, nephew?

Children: I am fine.

Relative: how's your study going on? In which class do you study?

Children: Fine uncle, and now I am in 10th standard.

Relative: Okay, son, take your seat.

Relative asks the parents, so what is the next plan for your child.

Parent replies: Nothing, see what happens after class 12th?

Relative: It means you do not have any target so far?

Parent replies: Will see, what we have to do, we have just like a simple living.

Relative: What about children?

Parents: If they have the capability, they can earn themselves.

Relative: Ok, Fine as you wish, please permit me to go.

Now, look at this conversation. Parents are so irresponsible; they do not have any plan for their children's future.

In the above conversation, we can see that the parents, who are not encouraging, are busy in conversation. If these children have a good school or society, there is only a fifty percent chance of making a promising career. Because parents are not responsible, children will learn this irresponsibility from parents. So the future of children will depend upon the gods.

How can parents improve this mistake?

First One: If parents are not interested in motivating their children to high thinking, they need to find a good school for their children and a mentor. Today's many extra curriculum activities run in society; Parents can get their children admitted there.

Second: Parents should listen to children about what they want to do after joining the different activity institutes.

You should not be a detractor if you can not encourage your children. I remembered a theory, If you can not become a good mentor, do not detractor. Like this theory, if you can not give children high thinking, you do not have any right to provide them with narrow thinking.

Now come and let see the second conversation.

Second Conversation (17.1)

This conversation is between a son and a father. The father is a Shopkeeper (Family Business). And when his child passes out from 12th standard, he goes to his father and shows interest in the Musical domain.

What is his father's reply? Let see.

Son: Daddy, I have passed my class, now I will have to decide my future.

Father: So what decides? Do not waste your time; come to the shop, sit here, and take over your family business.

Son: I do not want to sit here with you. I want to do something interesting in my life.

Father: Did you mean our family business is boring for you?

Son: No, it is not my mean.

Father: I know everything, come and join our family business.

Son: Daddy, I want more time for my dreams.

Father: What will you be earning? In the melodic line?

Son: Daddy, I'll manage both business and my music together.

Father: No, no success, you will run your business in this line.

Son: Give me one chance.

Father: Ok, do as you want to do, do not ask me anything.

Son: But daddy, listen to me.

Father: Do not talk to me.

In the above conversation, there is no conclusion coming out. And on the other hand, misunderstanding occurs between Father and Son. So how can we solve this issue?

First, Father should understand that every person can choose their happy career. And every person has different hobbies and skills. And I think if you make your hobby a job, you can not fail. A reason is standing behind this thought if you give a hundred percent to any work, you cannot slip up.

Son: Daddy, I have passed my class, now I will have to decide my future.

Father: Ok, so what is your decision for the next turn?

Son: I do not want to sit here with you; I want to do something interesting in my life.

Father: Ok, so tell me, how can I help you, son?

Father: I'll try to make your dreams come true.

Son: Daddy, I want to become a musician.

Son: Give me one chance!

Father: Do you know in this line challenging work is required? Can you do that?

Son: I am not sure, Daddy; I'll try my best.

Father: Ok, you can try for this, but one condition is that I do not want to see any Negligence.

Son: Yes, daddy.

Father:ok, best of luck, beta!

Father: Dear son, you can go for your dreams. If you fail there, then no need to worry, you can run your family business, and I am here to run this business till you come.

Son: I'll give my total effort in my passion, daddy, you do not worry (Happy).

In the above conversation, we can see a conclusion come out, and there is no misunderstanding. Both respect the feelings of each other. It is called the healthy conversation.

Now back to the main point, how this conversation encourages high thinking, the father is offering a big deal with their son. Father is encouraging to son for high consideration.

Father is not imposing the family business on his son. He respects his son's views and gives them a chance to achieve their goals. Father gave him a condition so that he would not think of negligence.

Now let's see the third conversation; in this conversation, the father encourages his son to achieve a good position in life.

Let's start; the father is a low-grade employee in the government sector, his son is intelligent in the study and passed out the 12th standard with good marks. Father always gave high thinking examples of legends to his son. That's why his son was motivated by the views of his father.

Now see the conversation (17.2)

Son: I have passed the 12th class and got good marks.

Father: Yes, I am proud of you, but I'll be happy more when you get your life goal. So what do you want to be next?

Son: I want to join a job and want to assist you.

Father: My dear son, you have to rise to the top.

Son: yes, daddy!

Father: You do not need to worry about anything; I'll support you in every way.

Son: Yes, daddy, I will achieve more with your support.

Son: I'll prepare for a higher job.

It is a normal conversation, and we can see the father is supporting his son morally. It's not all done in a day, and the father makes a foundation from the initial stage of the son's life.

So we will have to remember that we should make a foundation from the initial stage of childhood. If the foundation is weak, then the child can not be stable, and when he becomes young, he will feel directionless.

Parents should try to think high, and then they can transfer their thinking to children.

>>CHAPTER 18<<

INCONSISTENT DISCIPLINING

Inconsistent word is a theatrical word because we use this word for those who can not make one decision (thing). Inconsistency makes children mad because parents change their minds often, don't take a stand, and have difficulty making decisions. They will give excuses for this behavior, like tired, busy, mood off, etc.

Inconsistent parents make big mistakes to teach discipline to children. They have not good planing for discipline training. I think they would be confused about teaching discipline.

For example,A child is watching television, and his mother gives permission to watch for 30 minutes; after 30 minutes mother switched off the TV. The next day, the child is watching TV again, but now the watching time limit is crossed still TV is open because the mother is busy on the mobile phone. And the child is watching TV continuously. She forgets to switch off the TV or forgets to instruct the child to switch off the TV.

Next Day

The child is watching TV, and the mother is yelling, switch off the TV. You have completed 30 minutes.

Next Day

Mother and child are watching the movie for 3 hrs because their famous film is coming on TV.

The next day in the same situation, sometimes attending guests, sometimes she feels tired, sometimes she is busy.

In this example, the mother makes a time/schedule for the child, but she is not reviewing it properly, which is called discipline inconsistency.

The side effect of this Inconsistency

- The child will ignore your rules.

- The child will never take you seriously.

- The child will never scare of you.

- The child will cry to fulfill their wish.

Inconsistency behavior is also part of bad parenting, the mind of a child is to experience new things, and when a child sees this behavior, then he will be stubborn. He will cry for his stubbornness.

Let's read the conversation to understand better about disciplining inconsistently.

Conversation First 18.0 (Inconsistent behavior)

A father is going to school to admit their child, and he has already searched for other schools to accept their child. Let see what happens?

Father: Dear son, this school is good for you, take admission here. I have decided that you will do well here.

Son: Yes, Daddy.

Father: You can visit your school, and I will talk with the principal.

Son: Yes, I am excited, daddy!

Father: Ok, move.

Son is watching the playground and watching the children happy and playing. In his mind, he had set an image of this school.

Father: Son, come here, and let's go home. I have finalized your school.

Son: Thank you, daddy.

Next day

Son: Daddy, I want to buy my new shoes and school uniform.

Father: No, I'll search for a new school for you.

Son: But why daddy?

Father: No, this school is not suitable for you; go and play.

Son: Ok, daddy (Sad Tone).

Mother to Father: What happened? Why did you change your plan?

Father: My colleagues are saying this school is not good.

Mother: But my friend said the school is good and reputed.

Father: No, I'll search for another school.

Son is listening and feeling sad because the child had knitted dreams with the school. Now, the father is canceling his decision, which is not fair.

When a child doesn't know what will happen because parents perform inconsistently, the child may feel confusion, anxiety, and distrust. Inconsistency behavior will confuse your child and will develop your negative image.

How to improve this conversation

Parents should have already known about the school, and if this school is not good, then the father should not go there with his son, should have gone alone there.

See the child's happiness, do not trust what others are saying.

How should this conversation be healthy?

Father: A school is in my mind for our son.

Mother: Ok, Good, which school and have you visited the school?

Father: XY higher secondary school is in my mind.

Mother: You should visit first and ask about it from others.

Father: you are right; I'll go tomorrow.

Mother: Ok

The next Day father is visiting school

Father: I want to visit school. I want to admit my son to school.

In the evening

I visited the school

Mother: Hows is the school environment?

Father: Everything is good, and other people are saying this school is not good.

Mother: I have also talked to my relative she says the school is good.

Father: I see the school record and find it suitable. So I think once we should go with the son to school.

Mother: Yes, that is good.

Father: Dear son, come here.

Son: Yes, daddy.

Mother: Son, your father visited a school for your admission.

Father: So we decided that you will visit the school tomorrow.

Son: Yes, daddy.

Mother: I'll also come with you.

Son: I like this school, and I'll study here.

Mother: You will be comfortable here.

Parents: Ok, let's come back home.

At night same day

Son: Daddy, I am happy!

Father: Yes, I hope you will study well.

Son: Daddy, I'll study well. I want a new bag and uniform.

Father: Sure, dear, we will buy it soon.

In this conversation, you can see the child is happy because there is no confusion in his family. The parents are standing on same decision, and parents went to the school with the children, that is a plus point.

Inconsistency behavior creates a toxic environment in the family, which will make you mad and aggressive. The child's mind is new and learning more things day by day, and if parents are not on one decision, the child will be confused. And in any confusion, you can not do any work with perfection. So parents should teach the perfection-model to children.

What are the reasons for inconsistent behavior?

I am giving some common reasons for this behavior.

- **Low self-confidence.**

- **Depend upon others.**

- **Laziness.**

- **Solipsistic personality.**

- **Fear.**

- **Lack of knowledge.**

- **Immature Parents.**

- **No worry for the future.**

- **Toxic parents.**

- **Misunderstanding between parents.**

- **Not interested in children.**

- **Lack of management.**

- **Too busy life.**

- **Health issues.**

Conversation Second 18.1 (Disciplining Inconsistently)

A mother is teaching discipline to her daughter. She is making the schedule for her daily routine, like yoga, lunchtime, watching TV, studying, etc., and her daughter's nickname is Eddy. So come and see what's the conversation is going on between mother and eddy.

Mother: Eddy, I am going to make your daily schedule.

Eddy: Ok, mom.

Mother: I have fixed your TV watching time is 3 to 4 PM daily.

Mother: Study Time and homework time is 4 to 6 PM.

Mother: Your playing time is 6 to 7 PM.

Mother: Your reading time is morning 5 to 6 AM.

Mother: As the schedule is as follows.

- Breakfast- 8 to 9 AM.

- Lunch- as per school time.

- Dinner – 8 to 8.30 PM.

- Sleeping time – 9.30 PM to 5 AM.

- Your Yoga time is 7 to 7.30 AM.

Mother: Eddy, You can learn your schedule to avoid any confusion.

Now, after making schedules, what will be happened? The First Thing we should remember, before making any rule, you should follow first.

First Day of schedule

Mother: Wake up, Eddy, time of the study.

Eddy: Yes, Mom, I am going to study.

Mother: OK, you will have to follow the Yoga schedule after that.

After some time

Eddy: My study completed, Mom!

Mother: Good, come and do yoga.

In evening time- Time to Watching TV

Mother and Eddy are watching TV, enjoying; Mother is saying, "Watch TV only for one hour." After that, you will follow the following schedule as I told you.

Eddy: Yes, Mom, I'll do as you say.

The first-day schedule has been completed. Now, what happened in next day? Let see

Eddy thinks: Mom is not waking up so far. It means I can enjoy my sweet dream.

Mom: Eddy, Have you woken up?

Eddy: No, I wake up with you.

As you can see, this schedule is disturbed for today, and this disturbing is going on daily. So Eddy could not follow the program, so she would not take her mother earnestly.

Mother could not maintain consistency; I am not saying that mother should be perfect. Many problems can come to disturb your schedule. But if you want to become a good parent, you will have to avoid this difficulty or find an alternative way.

>>CHAPTER 19<<

ARGUING IN FRONT OF CHILDREN

Arguments between the parents are common in the family. However, one or two arguments with your partner will not ruin your child forever. But if you are doing this daily, it will destroy your child. In the arguments of parents, many hurtful words come from the mouth. And these types of terms children can adopt. Once toddlers develop language skills, they mimic the language and communication styles of the surrounding adults. It can include word selection, tone, and volume. The Toddlers will show you how they interpret the arguments by speaking to others while angry. If the Arguments do it again and in front of children, children might display difficulties with concentration, have anxiety, or develop behavioral problems.

In the nuclear family, it is widespread. Most of the parents do arguments in front of children. Because children are always living with them, disputes can turn into the parents' fight, which will affect the child more. Want to see how?

Read this conversation (19.0)

Husband and wife watching TV, and child is completing homework. Suddenly, the child asks to sharpen the pencil. So, let see.

Child: Please sharpen my pencil. Its tip broke.

Please say to your mother beta (husband said).

Wife: You know already, I am going for cooking. (Wife Said).

Husband: I am tired.

Wife: It is not hard work. You can do it quickly.

Husband: If you seem easy to work, you should do it.

Wife: So what is difficult to sharpen the pencil?

Husband: I am also saying the same thing.

Wife: You are going to be lazy day by day.

Husband: Wah! Wah! I work in the office the whole day, and you taunt me at home.

Wife: It does not taunt. It is the truth.

Husband: Do not talk to me.

Wife: you never spend time with your child.

Husband: Do not teach me my fatherhood.

Wife: It is necessary to teach you.

After a few minutes, this argument turns into a fight. The child has stopped their work and staring at the face of mother and father. But parents are not taking care of their children. They are continuously bombarding words to each other. The child is feeling sad and learning some bad words also. How can you control this argument? I suggest some points help you manage the fight in front of children.

Listen to your partner carefully

You might feel your partner is entirely to blame, but you won't get a solution like this. Experts say it's essential to allow your partner to share their thoughts in a nonjudgmental environment before responding.

Keep on track

Don't start talking about one issue and focus on another matter.

Weigh before saying anything

Use phrases like "I think" and "I feel." these phrases will help your partner understand where you're coming from? It's also less threatening, shows vulnerability, and allows for engagement rather than making the other person feel attacked.

Focus on your breathing

Breathing will indicate that you are going to be hyper.

"Work on your breathing." keep calm," says Mansfield.

It will help you not lose your temper and get hyper, allowing you to be more in control of your emotions.

Look towards the kids

When you feel you are going on the wrong track, once, you should look at your child. The child face will change your restless mind into a tranquil mind.

Understand your responsibility

Most of the time, irresponsibility generates arguments. So every family member should understand their responsibility. In the nuclear family, duty will be more.

>>CHAPTER 20<<

FIGHTING IN FRONT OF CHILDREN

Whether parents fighting will harm young kids depends on its frequency, intensity, context, and how it does resolve. As I told in the above article, maybe one or two fights or arguments do not harm your child. But if the frequency does repeat, it will hurt your child.

How parent's fights will affect the children?

Insecurity in the mind of Children

Fighting will damage children's sense of security about the family's stand. Children exposed to a lot of arguments may worry about separation. Children worry about the silent treatment of one parent. It can make it challenging for them to have a sense of normalcy since fights may be inconstant.

It can affect the parent-child relationship.

High-conflict situations are stressful for parents, and they might not spend a lot of time with their children.

They can not care for children. They can not provide proper guidance to children as well.

The child will give less respect to parents. Maybe he made a negative image of his parents. The child will refuse the order of the parents. He will not share personal things with his parents.

It can create a stressful environment.

Overhearing frequent or severe fighting is stressful for every child. Stress can affect their physical and psychological health and interfere with normal, healthy development.

In a stressful environment, children will lose many things in their childhood.

- Happiness.

- Parents Care.

- Love from parents.

- Proper Guidance.

- Mental Peace.

When will this fight become problematic?

Then the child will affect by these symptoms.

- **The child is in Depression.**

- **Scare in sleep.**

- **Eating Disorders.**

- **Physical Issues.**

- **Sleep problems.**

- **Stomachaches or headaches.**

- **You are not answering correctly.**

- **Emotionally going weak**

******